M.F.K. FISHER

A Cordiall Water

A Garland of Odd & Old Receipts
to Assuage the Ills of
Man & Beast

North Point Press
San Francisco
1981

For
Eleanor Kask Friede

Preface

Sometimes people ask me what I think is the best book I have written. My only answer is that I have never been satisfied. But, as things now stand, I feel that my translation of Brillat-Savarin's PHYSIOLOGY OF TASTE (which of course I did not *write*), and A CORDIALL WATER are perhaps the pick of the litter.

The reason I like this little book about folk medicine is that its prose seems to have a purity about it that I have long sensed in writers who are thinking in two languages. I never tried to attain this. Joseph Conrad had it, and so did Nabokov and other greater workers than I could ever be. But for a few hours, while I was writing about horny cats and aching bones and nosebleeds, and all that clutter of life, I was stripped of banality, and I wrote simply in my native tongue, because I was temporarily detached from it and thus more aware.

In about 1960 my two daughters and I were living into our fourth year in Aix-en-Provence. They left for their classes before eight, and came back after six at night. They worked hard, and so did I. We had two rooms on the fifth floor of the old Hotel de Provence, and we met for lunch on the Cours Mirabeau and sat for a couple of hours, eating lightly. At night, because the hotel had no restaurant, we scrounged happily around town.

So while my girls dug into Racine and Giono I tidied some mental drawers about folk medicine, and what I wrote in the quiet room above the rooftops of the old town came out as this little book. I believe that it has a pleasant honesty of style, and I hope I am not mistaken.

M. F. K. Fisher
Glen Ellen, 1980

A Cordiall Water

Introduction

We have medicines to make women speak; we have none to make them keep silence.

Anatole France

This book is a collection of odd and old receipts to cure the ills of people and animals, mostly told to me by the believers.

There is no doubt that much of what we know of medicine comes from very ancient times, and from the birds and animals that we have watched. Myself, I do not know enough to say how or why one certain weed will calm a fever in a sick dog or antelope, nor can I guess what tells the beasts about that weed, any more than I can recite the new fine names for its magical components on a box of costly fever pills from a modern laboratory. All I can do is wonder, and everything that I have remembered and recorded here has made me do that.

It is easy to paraphrase a good saying, and the better

the saying, the easier . . . as well as the harder to disguise. I could not presume to hide the fact that I am deliberately misquoting George Orwell's deathless motto about equality when I state that all books are written with a purpose but some with less purpose than others. This book of odd restoratives and remedies started with almost none, unless it was to put some order in my desk as well as my thoughts.

For a long time I have been noting strange things people have told me about illness and health. And recipes in old books would startle me by their foolishness and their faith; labels from old bottles and pillboxes, and clippings from newspapers, collected as if by themselves . . . and suddenly, in a move from one place to another, I saw that I had a disordered drawerful spilling from the table, fluttering in my thoughts. Innate tidiness stepped in, at least to help me make room for more.

At first I was interested as to why I had thought this or that hoarded note was worth its paper, and if there seemed no answer, it was thrown away.

Then I was astonished and dismayed to realize my growing confusion about how to classify all the cuttings and scribbled comments which I had collected for so many years with such careless compulsion. When does the ounce of prevention that is said to be worth a pound of cure stop being preventive and become restorative? What is the difference, then, between a cure and a remedy? Semantic dangers menaced me, and I groaned in the trap I had sprung on myself, as words like panacea and drug and nostrum took on sharper, meaner outlines.

Who can say, still, whether Mother Periwinkle's Miracle Salve is a nostrum, a piece of arrant quackery, or a bit of instinctive folk medicine? Where, most of all, is the fine line that separates scientific from religious healing?

It has been exciting to knit into some kind of pattern all these "phisical receipts," as the old cookery books called them, and while I have found it impossible, for instance, to keep all the ones with liquor in them apart from the ones concerning alcoholic as well as actual snakebite, still I have managed with some license to separate the sheep from the men, and even the men from the mandrakes.

Best of all, I have made a few things clearer to myself, at least.

One is that we have long known and used much that the birds and beasts have taught us.

Another is that the great difference between our folk medicine and theirs is that we need, being men, to mix faith with our healing. We need to trust something unknown, and to count on more than the actuality of a potion in the cup, a pill on the tongue.

Animals go without any mystical query to the water or mud or herb that will help them, and as far as we can tell they do not question their going, nor pray to be led, nor offer thanks when they are better. Neither do they need our aid, except of course when we have caged and domesticated them past their own help. But we need them and learn ceaselessly from them.

All this is good to realize. It seems to bring natural order and even common sense into our acceptance of medical help, so that, being men, we can concoct trust-ingly from an Elizabethan herbal a drink which animals would create within themselves by eating various roots and flowers and leaves. *We believe* its claims, which al-though perhaps somewhat longer than others made in this little book of mine, are in reality not much different from them:

> To Make a Cordiall Water good against any Infections, as ye Plague, Poxe, Measles, burning feaver, & to remove any of-fensive or Venemouse Matter from ye Hart or Stomach, or to be used after surfetts or in Passion of ye Mother, or for Children in fitts of Convulsions, & is generally Good to Comfort or strengthen Nature.

I

Be favorable to bold beginnings.
Virgil

From the first it has been as puzzling for me as it is for most people to separate myth and religion from medical reality.

There was a little stranger in the second grade, a quiet child who came and then went away without leaving any friends except perhaps me. I remember her always, though, for two good reasons.

She lived in a house that still haunts me pleasurably, a wooden shack built and abandoned by early California Mexicans, with their bare pressed earth around it instead of grass, and cactuses along the edge of the plot in a ferocious and noble fence, and eucalyptus trees rearing airy-fairy above it as they used to there. This place was away from our prim town, up a dirt road and into a little canyon, and it seemed enviably romantic to me to think, when I saw Bertha slip in her gray, silent way into the classroom, that she had come down the deserted dusty road, so different from sidewalks, and had closed behind her the door of the shack that I had often spied on from higher in the hills because it was so much more beautiful than the straight houses we lived in.

And she wore around her neck a bag of "assafeddity."

Its rank garlicky smell was perhaps what first drew me to her. It reminded me a little of my half-Mexican friend Gracie. I missed her that year. She was temporarily away from Whittier while her father was in jail again or her mother had another baby or something like that. Gracie had a very strong, fine smell, predominantly garlic and to me seductively unlike the pale odor of bath powder of the little girls I was supposed to play with. But Bertha's smell was not healthy like Gracie's.

It had a bitterness to it, rather rancid, and when I discussed this casually with my mother, she laughed in a vague remembering way and said to see if my new friend did not wear a little cloth bag hanging under her dress around her neck. And so she did. During recess we went down to the dim toilets together, and quietly she showed it to me . . . gray gray . . . even her skin in that light was the color of her woolen dress, her underwear, the soft little bag like a dead field mouse on a string.

The smell was stifling, but I sniffed deeply of it, so foreign to everything I had been taught to accept as Only.

It would keep away fevers, she whispered gently to

me. It would protect her, because, and she bade me come very close to see, it was in a little sack on which there smiled, through the grime, the printed face of the Virgin Mary. It has been blessed, Bertha said, and she slipped the foul-smelling thing out of sight again.

I felt puzzled but reassured, perhaps because she was so sure about it. I reported to my mother that yes, it was "assafeddity" all right, but for reasons which I did not wonder about then, I forgot to say anything about the picture of the Blessed Virgin, and we agreed laughingly that surely no disease would get past that rank cloud of garlic . . .

We were wrong, for soon Bertha died, and her family moved silently away from the house in the canyon. I did not bother much about it; I was very busy that year, and had never really played with Bertha except at recess. But I began to wonder passively about things like the power of prayer, and why such medicine as the assafetida did not help, even with the Virgin's blessing.

It was about then that I discovered, in the revolving bookcase in my father's office at the *News*, a strange cloth-bound copy of *Nostrums and Quackeries*. I should like to have it again, or at least know where it went to. As I remember the feel of it, it was not like ordinary books, being larger and heavier, with pages of glossy paper, most probably, I now think, a "vanity press" publication of the life work of some forgotten crackpot who was willing to spend everything to expound his theory.

In this case, angrily (most such people are angry) and lavishly (often such people are rich or can find money), every popular patent medicine consumed in the United States was "exposed" as fraudulent, dangerous, and above all ridiculous. So were things like electric belts and magnetized gloves and iron rings. The scorn in the book even covered such cripplers as corsets, high heels, "bust developers," and "complexion waxes." It ripped with a sneer through baby foods, virility tonics, magic liniments, hair restorers, female restoratives, and pills guaranteed to do fascinating things like grow third sets of teeth and make warts vanish forever. And it was illustrated. On almost every page was a clear, sharp cut of an advertisement for one of the nostrums under fire, and my knowledge of both the human figure and typography perhaps reached full growth during the two or three years that I devoted to the marvelous book.

I read it only on Sunday afternoons. During that period in the family life, my mother was busy having a new set of children, and to quiet down the general *brouhaha* of the weekends, my father would disappear with my sister and me to the deserted and echoing silence of the newspaper plant. It impregnated us forever with the tantalizing itching excitement of any place in the world where newsprint is . . . the cold smell of ink, with its indescribable bite . . . the mystery of paper . . .

Everything was dead on Sundays, of course, and until Father lighted one or two bulbs in the Front Room we stuck close to him, and then past the four linotypes in the Back Room to the Paper Room. Once there we felt safe and sure again, as he returned to his little office past the still hulks of the two presses. Sometimes he turned on more lights, and hovered over the job presses and the one hand press that he insisted on keeping, but mostly he was gone for the afternoon as far as we knew or cared.

The Paper Room was a kind of box built in the cavern of the Back Room, about twelve feet square and with its own roof and its walls screened on the top third, presumably to keep out rats. For us it kept out everything: dark, silence, cold.

Except for the door, it was solid shelves, all piled tidily with the most magical assortment of papers of every size, color, thickness, and, above all, smell. We never touched any of it, except for the piles of scrap on the shelf nearest the big table with its lethal cutter, but before he left us our father would deftly pull off two pieces of onionskin, a sheet of this, another of that . . .

We drew, wrote letters, made paper boats and pigeons as we had once learned from a Japanese houseboy named Amimoto. And as I read from *Nostrums and Quackeries,* which I had quickly learned to flick from its shelf on the revolving bookcase as we passed through our father's office, I became conscious of many things besides the plain foolishness of mankind in believing in such promises as all the bottle labels made, and I began a lasting curiosity about how and why and when fears and fevers went together.

It was plain that neither the stinking powdered resin in little Bertha's greasy pouch nor the pretty picture on it had kept her from dying. Yet countless people kept on looking for a power, any power, to cure them of more pains than I had dreamed of! Some illnesses, I grew to see, were as much of the spirit as of the body, but trust as well as hope would keep on making enough cures to keep even the silliest nostrums flourishing.

That was when my skepticism about much of what we call the art of medicine was born, I suppose, and my suspicion of such things as "miracle drugs" and my impatience with our bland acceptance of them. And from this skepticism and all the rest of it grew my consciousness of the basic simplicity of caring for the human body, mostly learned by us over the centuries from the animals we live with, and from the peasants and farmers who care for them.

Cows and dogs and even very young strong humans, given a chance, will take care of themselves when they are unwell. Often their cures are as simple as sleep, warmth, and fasting. When they seek out grasses and herbs to chew, unfettered instinct will lead them to the ones that modern science duplicates in powder or pills or hypodermic form: minerals, acids, salts, and sugars in polysyllabic formulae.

Science often helps people to help animals, certainly; and in return the wisest of the scientists learn much about simplicity from the bee, the fox, the horse, and from the farmers who for centuries have lived close to them. There is reason, they see, in all the sweats, the fasts, the purges and lotions and teas of folk medicine.

The remedies, then, that I have considered for one reason or another in this book: I would not attempt to make scientific explanations of them, any more than I would presume to outline their spiritual worth or lack of it. All I can do is what I have done since I was young, listening to Bertha's soft voice in the girls' toilet, reading to myself in the Paper Room about human sickness and credulity—accept the fact that it is impossible to separate their folly and mysticism from human life and death.

The Virgin Mary did not save my little friend from an early death. Neither did the fetid sack about her neck. But we go right on using assafetida, even today and even in the great laboratories, for curative powers which have nothing to do with its primitive stink, just as we continue to believe in our various gods whatever their names and images. And we continue to learn from the beasts of the earth, the air, the sea, who cure themselves without spiritual dependence.

There is no point in trying to follow, for my own possible satisfaction, any kind of chronology in this list of simple remedies, now that I see that they began with Bertha's "assafeddity" and my acceptance of the fact that medicine, even when mixed with religion, will not always work. It was fortunate, or so I feel, that I could offset this possible shock by an intensive and graphic education in human faith in the book about nostrums. How ridiculous the promised cures all prove to be . . . and how strong our natures, to continue to believe in them!

II

I had most need of blessing, and
   "Amen"
Stuck in my throat.

Shakespeare

When I was little, my grandmother lived with us, or vice versa, and she prescribed a few remedies which I see now were from her years of life on the prairies that later became the state of Iowa. And yet they were no more American than Brazilian, say, and while they are less used now than they used to be in the settled parts of the world, ones like them are still potential life-savers in remote settlements almost everywhere.

One of them, perhaps the most disagreeable, was for sore throats and coughs, and for just that, Grandmother kept in her medicine closet a rolled strip of outing flannel pinned tight with a diaper pin and furred on the edges from much use.

It was of a disagreeable yellowish color and let off an

unfading odor of camphorated oil that was unpleasant
only because of its association with the treatment:

> Rub the throat with warmed oil, and wrap well with the
> strip of flannel which has been soaked in hot water and
> wrung dry. Then [*and this was what really seemed most hateful*]
> cover the steaming compress with a long black cotton
> stocking.

All schoolchildren wore such equipment in those
days, and to my sister and me there was something inde-
scribably embarrassing about being seen with black
stockings on our long skinny legs and the same thing
wrapped about our throats. We pretended to feel and
sound worse than we were, just to stay home from classes
in this odious travesty, and before we grew too old we
had made our mother understand our pain, so that
Grandmother seldom succeeded in trapping us into her
bathroom if we sounded croaky. But she kept the roll of
dingy oil-soaked old flannel until she died, in case we
should turn sensible and let her swathe us.

(Indeed, when I had my tonsils removed, as was the
easy and dangerous fashion then, she stated firmly that if
I had but worn a compress now and then when I needed
one, such a foolhardy interference with Nature might
have been avoided. And by now there is much scientific
agreement with her protest . . .)

Long after this dubious victory against my grandam's
simple medicine, I was sipping a delicious drink which
would have made every teetotaling cell in her body whirl
in horror, if she still had a body at all, and talking in a

lavishly innocent California version of a Tahitian hut, air-conditioned of course, with its owner, who had been raised, mostly with no hut at all, in a Brazilian village. When we got to the subject of sore throats, with the alcoholic logic of any such conversation, and I outlined the horrid Family Cure, he grew excited and happy.

"Exactly, exactly," he said. "Iowa. California. The Amazon. But a few slight differences. Yes, a little boy in that Brazil has a sore throat, very bad. He cannot speak. No flannel of course, but always there is a sock or two in the village. And this perhaps would shock your grandmother. No hot smelly oil, no hot water even. All that is needed in that sock is sweat, real plenty of *sweat*. So it must be a dirty sock, in fact filthy. Ah, then what a fast cure, what a warm healthy smell!"

It was even easier to go on from there, our older throats lubricated inwardly by our drinks, cold, unhealthy, and delightful. We agreed more and more happily on everything to do with folk medicine, and when he would say, "There is no doubt about it, purifications from freshly killed pigeons are the same in Haiti as in Provence," I would agree solemnly. And when I asserted, "Animals know more spring tonics than any biochemist does," he backed me up with ponderous joy.

We matched story for story, and more remedies were garbled into universal cure-alls in that pseudo-Tahitian hut than have ever been used singly by suffering man, I think. It did no harm, and I felt better to learn that somebody else had once worn a sock about his aching throat, for the same reason, even though the smell was different.

III

Later I thought of the animals we had lauded so grandly for being wiser than most men, and I remembered things I had heard and read about their self-cures, and about our attempts to help them. As a matter of course, I thought of Blackberry . . .

He was without doubt the rarest of many wonderful cats who have lived with me. I remember too many things about him, so that it is hard to talk of only one now: the way he healed himself after a mighty battle, really three times, for he waged four of them in as many years before he died after the last one.

This was when he was old for his race, because he was peculiar in that until he was almost nine he would have none of love and its warfare.

Females wooed him at least twice a year, and fought

each other noisily to excite some interest in him, but he paid no attention except to yawn. I wondered about this, and with some regret, for he would have made a good father. He was beautiful, with fine but strong bones, small ears, a daintiness that was not effeminate, and great skill in hunting.

In the spring he loved to dance on the lawn with butterflies, who seemed to know that he did not intend to catch them and so would fly low and then up and past his deliberate frolickings.

Then when he was almost nine, and I was convinced that he had been born a feline eunuch, he went into such a passion for a little female kitten as I had never seen before. She was too young for him. I had to separate them, or he would have torn her to pieces a hundred times a day, blindly. It was sad and terrible. He was literally burning to death, and turned from a silky long-haired tranquil beauty to a wild-eyed snarler. He would not eat, and could not sleep.

Finally I gave away the bewildered and innocent kitten, thinking to calm him. Instead he ran away, no doubt to look for her, and I who had grown used to his tabbiness was forlorn for him.

In a week he came back, a shadow but quiet, and that year almost every kitten born in the Valley was Blackberry's, for when the moon was right he would leave again. Now and then one of his neglected wives would seek him out, and he would lead her away discreetly, being very gentlemanly in spite of his lost daintiness of manner.

Finally, though, after about a year of this sustained

libertinism, he returned to us in a most dreadful fashion.

I heard a small cheeping sound now and then, so like a bird's that I did not heed it at first. It came from the canyon, a narrow rocky place with a few straggly, ancient eucalyptus trees shading the muddy bottom, and for the knowing there were paintings on hidden and protected stones, done in the mysterious and ineradicable reddish stuff of ancient times, by Indians who came there to pray and be healed.

It was still said in the Valley that the water that trickled and in winter rushed down our canyon could be bottled and sold, for it would cure fevers and sores, and soothe pain, and in general was good for what ails one. Nobody, not even the modern Indians, did more than talk.

But down in that muddy slit in the hills lay the cat Blackberry, and his faint cheeping mews led me finally to him, after more than a day of searching through the rocks and reeds.

He lay so flat into the mud that I almost stepped on him, and he was stretched out so long and far that he looked more like the shape of a dead reptile than a living animal. The mud was so coated on his fur that it was cracked in the dry air. I could not tell which end was the head of the horrid dead-alive thing, until he made another faint cry and I saw the feeble opening of his caked lips.

I bent over him, really sick with shock. Such beauty once, now dying surely in this abject state . . . It was a shame, a shame, and I could hardly bear it.

I started to touch him, and then I felt what was like a bell ringing, or a flash blinding me, a warning as clear as any shout: I was not to put my hand on him.

I crouched above him for some time, and realized with a kind of awe that he was ripped from head to tail, and that in with the caked mud his flesh was mixed as it hung in strings from his skeleton. His mouth stayed open, with his tongue loosely hanging from it, and an occasional breath lifted his ribs almost invisibly. His eyes stayed closed. I withdrew, with farewell in my heart, for surely he was dying, and I seemed to have been told to let him do so alone.

The next day I went down to get his body. Of course it was not there, but a few feet further down the stream bed, and still living. When Blackberry heard me he mewed again, and again I bent over him, to see that he had dragged himself that far and that he lay with his other side in the black mud. Still I did not touch him, but I hurried back up the canyon for a pinch of ground meat and a flat saucer of water for him. Hours later they were still untouched, but his mew of recognition seemed stronger to me, and he had turned himself over again.

In the next week I watched a miraculous healing take place. When the caked mud fell off him and he rolled into wetter places I could see with horror that his flesh did indeed hang in strings, and many of his bones and tendons were laid bare. How he continued to exist I could not understand, for he ate nothing and never touched water for about eight days. Then he ate three or four times a day a bit of lean chopped meat which I left beside him, and his eyes opened and looked at me with what seemed thoughtfulness and amusement.

In about three more days he arose, licked himself stiffly, and walked up the canyon in easy stages to the house. He was a pitiful sight, but dignified.

A month of rest and genteel spoiling had him fine and sleek again . . . until the next year and the next, and finally the fourth such bout, which at first seemed to me the result of his tackling a wildcat or a lynx. Then I saw that three common Toms from the Valley must have attacked him together, to avenge his general seduction of all their females . . . for sensing him to be old, they dared follow him this time up to the muddy bottom of the canyon, where he had dragged himself after God knows how long a battle down in the Valley. There they finished him off.

I have told a few people about this and they have not quite believed me, but I know it because I saw the end of it happen. I beat them away (it was their howls that drew me, for Blackberry made not a sound), but this time he was dead.

It was as well. Even the black mud of the Indian's healing stream could not have hung his legs back on his frame, his head on his neck. It did, though, keep him alive for the last wildly productive years of his long life, and now almost every cat for miles around has some of his strain in it.

One thing that has always interested me is that during the first three times Blackberry lay in the mud and let the hair and flesh grow back, no enemies ever came to bother him. But when he was old, and plainly not a match any more for them, they got him . . . and I think that not only the Toms, but probably almost any of the animals he had long hunted, would have come then, the fourth time he was downed, to get even with him.

IV

Pleased to the last, he crops the
  flowery food,
And licks the hand just raised to shed
  his blood.

Alexander Pope

It has never really been agreed that cats are domesticated animals, and perhaps Blackberry's knowledge of
how to heal himself was a kind of link between the old
wild ways of the lion and the eagle, and the docile dependence upon us two-legged animals of the horse and
cow, the dog, the barnyard peckers.

Much that is told of the ways of untamed beasts must
stay hearsay and therefore legend, even in these days of
the snooping long-range camera; but hunters have sworn
for hundreds of years to certain things they *know*, mostly
about the wounded and the dying, and what they say
proves over again the truism that we have always looked
to the animals for wisdom in healing.

In 1300, an English monk noted in his daybook that

goats, like stags, will run when wounded to eat of the herb dittany. Far earlier, though, in Sparta and else-where, this wild plant was applied to the wounds of sol-diers, both as fresh leaves and in brews and ointments, and even now it is grown in some simple gardens to be dried for healing teas.

Bears, it is said, cure their sores by running and roll-ing in the soft woolly leaves of mullen patches . . . and that reminds me of a cure told me by a farmer in the dry hills of southern France, for man, not beast. He said that the most soothing and best cure for open wounds, and especially for burns and sores, was made with what we always call rabbit ears at home—silvery soft oblong leaves from a plant that grows close to the earth in dry country, perhaps a kind of sage (or mullen?). He said the velvety fur was soft against the sore, and full of healing juices.

"Pick them when long and at their prettiest," he said seriously to me, "and lay them flat in a wide-mouth jar, and then cover them with your best olive oil. They will last forever. When you need them, lay them flat against the burn or sore, and bind them on gently. Take off the bandage in forty-eight hours and you will see the perfect new skin, with never a scar. It is a miracle!"

I have been told that when a lion is ill he will hunt out a young monkey and eat it, and I can find no reasonable parallel for this in our own behavior (at the moment anyway!), but I do know that the simplest way to dis-gorge anything noxious, for us, is to do exactly what a lion does when he has eaten too much: he sticks his paw down his throat!

In the same way, when a bear knows that he has eaten something poisonous, like the mandrake, he will search out an anthill just as we use an emetic like mustard or soda, and eat the peppery acidic insects until he vomits. A lion probably would do the same, and find a weed to fill the purpose, for I have often watched cats eat certain grasses to make themselves throw up a poisonous lizard.

Dogs are perhaps less sensible, at least in their domesticated state, but they still work strange and wonderful cures by licking their own wounds. I have been told that there is a definite connection between the way they clean themselves of feces and disinfect the wounds, but I am too ignorant to try to explain why certain of the very active bacilli from their intestinal tract help to counteract infectious bacilli that might cause gangrene . . . Certainly it is plain that this instinctive licking in a dog, not considered at all "nice" by finicky owners, has saved many a fine animal from illness or death, and veterinarians are the first to say so. (A distasteful proof of man's mistaken imitation of this canine remedy is that many recipes for healing wounds in the Middle Ages included the tongues of puppies.)

Both animals and men change their eating habits with the seasons, although the latter are less obvious about it. These changes are basically a kind of preventive medicine. For instance, a layer of insulating fat will act, on any animal, as a protection against winter cold, and that is why, to our surprise and even apprehension, we find ourselves eating heavy meals in the first cold days of autumn. Most healthy people grow thicker, glossier hair then, too, just as the animals thicken their pelts in a more necessary over-all protection.

Natural mating seasons are more clear-cut among animals than with us, or at least we like to think so, but some of their results are common to both kingdoms, as when a female bird, like a robin, during the mating and laying season will peck at sea shells to get the minerals she will need to make her own. In the same way, pregnant women in regions where calcium is lacking in the regular diet, like the northern islands of Japan, are fed heavily with pigs' trotters and other gristly dishes . . . to make new bones, of course, not shells!

Cows, unlike cats, cannot continue some of their atavistic wanderings for the leaves and grasses they need for certain symptoms and seasons, and dairymen have long known that some acids should be added to the diets of both milch cows and bulls to insure strong, healthy, intelligent offspring. Farmers have done it for centuries by putting good cider vinegar or sour wine into the food, and of course modern laboratories manage to supply the basic potassium in much more complicated forms.

In an even more drastic and dramatic way, wild creatures like the minks, which are now grown on "ranches" for their pelts, have shown their prosperous captors that they miss the sour berries and leaves they seek out at certain times of the year. They have developed for themselves a tragicomic disease called Ménière's syndrome.

With it they suffer from acute dizziness. They reel and stagger. Finally, in order to hold themselves up, they try to support themselves by catching their own tails, which they bite so frantically that often they wear them down to a pitiful nub as they whirl about the cages. Then in March comes the worst part of this dervishlike malady: it is almost impossible for them to breed, because the males have lost the long helpful tail-brace they must use to set themselves during the mating . . . and they are too dizzy to stand up anyway.

To add to the miserable situation, the pastel minks which are most valuable to their growers are by nature the ones who carry their heads cocked to one side, so that when they do not get the acids they would normally find in wild berries, they are already in a perfect position to start whirling.

Fortunately folk medicine has suggested a remedy eagerly accepted by many mink ranchers, or whatever their trade name may be, and they stay free of both syndrome and nightmares by giving each of their minks a daily ration of one quarter of a teaspoon of cider vinegar or a more expensive chemical substitute . . . Now March comes undreaded. "Bright-eyed and bushy-tailed," every last mink able to walk a straight line, 1200 glossy skipping little females and 300 industriously erect males will produce without benefit of freedom a fine batch of some 3500 potential wage-earners for their canny owners!

V

We ought to learn from the kine one
thing: ruminating.

Friedrich Nietzsche

Just as we have complicated our own medications by
mixing them with superstition and faith and other attri-
butes of our religions, so we have added some of our
physical fancies to the nostrums that we give our beasts.
Perhaps we feel a kind of guilt for having removed them
from their first simplicity? Whatever the reason, we feel
obliged to compound prescriptions worthy of any laboratory for the sick animals we try to keep healthy.

A hot toddy for a man with a cold, for instance, is a
simple remedy and one that is age-old. In the same way,
in the fifteenth century, a farmer gave to his wheezing
cow or horse a bucket of sweetened warm ale. But even a
hundred years later, here is what the poor beast got, according to a manuscript of veterinary notes:

For a Cow or Mare Which having taken a Bad Cold refuseth also its food: Mix one ounce each of Grains of Paradise, Diaphoretic Antimony and Bay berries in powder, with 2 ounces of Gentian in powder. Stir into a quart of warm ale, with half a pound of Treacle or honey, and repeat as occasion may require, for three days.

I do not know the modern treatment for a rheumy cow, but I can state that men still rely on hot toddies, even compounded with liberal doses of whatever is most fashionable in antibiotics and/or other miracle drugs . . . and that both species continue to have colds.

It is not known, at least by me, whether snakes and fish suffer from this miserable affliction, but I have heard the theory, advanced in an argument against keeping bedroom windows open in winter, that the reason birds never sneeze or cough is that they sleep always with their heads tucked into their warm yet aerated wings. The common hen was cited as a prime example of this idyllic preventive.

I cannot advance any arguments for or against it since I do not really like birds, at least enough to live much with them, and I actively dislike chickens. Once when I was very young, though, a neighbor asked us to watch over her canary while she went away for a few days, and I have a strong and distinct feeling that I heard him cough several times before he died, soon after she left him with us. Cough or sneeze . . .

Cows, because we depend so much upon them for food, are a prime object of our medical attentions, and it is tempting to repeat some of the things I have read about the ways we fool them into giving us more milk, more calves . . . the way we make them live longer, and weigh more, and in general *be* more for our hungers. Certainly there is nothing much sadder than a herd of scrawny sick cattle, nor much prettier than a silky placid milch cow licking her handsome little calf; and just as certainly we know many ways to make and keep the good rather than the bad picture, for our own reasons. I shall content myself now with copying only two remedies, one I have read and remembered for its mysterious simplicity (which to me sounds quite hopeless), and one I have been told.

The first one is called "Mrs. Conder's Receipt for Cattle after the bite of a Mad Dog," first noted in 1694 in *The Receipt Book of Ann Blencowe:*

Wild mint, wild primrose roots, and English box: a little more of the box than of the other things.

How? Should the leaves be dried and powdered? Should they be mixed into a paste, or perhaps drunk in another of those quarts of warm ale? Should they be crushed, fresh from the meadows and the garden, and rubbed on the bitten places? Would not the cattle die anyway? It all seems too optimistic.

The second remedy sounds more realistic to me, perhaps because it is as old as man, almost, and is still used not only for cows but for women in remote places in the world like Sardinia, high Italian villages, even isolated farms in Provence. It might never have been written down, so natural is it, so full of generosity and thanks-giving.

> To Strengthen and Comfort a Cow after Calving Give her a loaf of fresh bread, soaked in a liter of good red wine.

Substitute Woman for Cow and Birthing for Calving . . . except that it is too easy for us, being human and therefore dependent upon a grain of complicating mysticism with our simplest medicine, to go on into the significances of the rebirth of our spirits through the bread and the wine. It takes great humility to link ourselves at one time with the patient cow and the Holy Sacrament. It is best perhaps to return to the recipe, and to recall that often in very poor farms a loaf of bread and a drink of "good red wine" are hard to come by, and therefore right for paying homage to one of the great mysteries.

VI

The toad beneath the harrow knows
Exactly where each tooth-point goes;
The butterfly upon the road
Preaches contentment to that toad.
Rudyard Kipling

Some people are able to claim that they have always felt a close personal relationship with everything about them, from the leaf on its twig to the fox and the fish in their haunts. I envy them, and know that it was a waste of time for me to take about twenty-three years to be able to recognize a toad as an important entity and not merely an adjunct to other life, including my own.

I was a young married woman when this happened. Meanwhile I had known a few toads, but always impersonally, during my fine childhood in the dusty hills of Whittier.

They were of only two kinds, for we did not have the ponds and streams that would have introduced me to the fat frogs and toads of another kind of country. There were

tiny tree toads, which were sometimes scarce and sometimes noisily plentiful. They could be caught and held
gently in one's hand, and their delicate throats went in
and out like the brain under the fontanelle in a baby's
skull. They did not sing while I held them.

And the other kind, the bigger dry ones which I
called horny-toads and caught in the hot sun when they
stood blinking on a rock or a path, never sang at all, nor
made any sound. They were supposed to enjoy an occasional insect, but although I have often kept one for several days in a shoebox by my bed and supplied it well
with flies, ants, and little beetles, I have never seen it
even look at one, much less taste the water in the screw-
top of a bottle which I always put beside it. A very few
times, after long staring at the strange dry silent creature, I have seen the flick of its tongue. This always startled me and gave me the feeling of having been granted a
special favor, so that when I took the horny-toad back to
the hills I put it down with gratitude upon the dust.

But even so, I never felt more than a protective curiosity about it and all the other toads I met, until I was
grown and had learned a little more. Then one day I was
astounded, in a naïve, innocent way really, to hear a respected older friend named Georges say in French to his
new son, "Thee's a handsome baby, my little toad."

I had never thought of the word, in any language at
all, as an endearment. Indeed, in my mother tongue it
was nearly the opposite, and to say that anyone resem-
bled a toad was cruel.

I knew Georges well enough to tell him of my astonishment, and he was amused, and the love and gaiety in his voice as he looked at the baby and talked about him made me want to feel the same way about children of my own, dear fat little toads hopping about . . .

Since that day I have felt a direct personal relationship with every frog and toad I have met, in music, in paintings and books, and on the road or the wet stone. I think their legs are very good to eat too, especially the tiny ones that used to seem to hop right from the canal near Dijon into the hot garlicky dish on my table beside the water. But I could not bear to kill one, and I always shudder to remember that one of my Swiss friends earned money in the summers, when he was a boy, by supplying a big mountain hotel with long, skinned frogs' legs.

He caught them by the hundreds, and made enough cash to go down to Lucerne to the government school for waiters and cooks, but he said that forever, when he was unwell or fatigued, he was haunted by the way the frogs would cross their delicate hands in prayer over their white bosoms, like dead girls in their coffins, as he held them tightly by the legs across the chopping block.

There are many legends about toads, all of them with some good reason behind them and some of them with folk medicine to add the impact of reality to the myth. These tailless animals, for instance, are supposed to be patient, and because of their clumsy fat shuffling pace along the ground were dried and powdered during the Middle Ages as a cure for nervousness and twitchings.

Sometimes the connection between the remedy and

its recipient is less obvious, and I do not know why frogs were used in a cure which I found in one of the fat volumes which used to be in every American kitchen or library, called something like *Dr. William Guthrie's Family Almanac and Household Compendium, Containing More Than 5000 Receipts, Games, Cures for All Sicknesses, and Anecdotes of Wholesome Merriment.* I forgot everything but the date—1865—of the shabby volume in which I turned up this remedy for coughs and "consumption":

It starts out, "Take the hind legs of fifty well-skinned green frogs . . ." and it is for a soup to be drunk warm at bedtime, then advising the cook to be sure to save the meat for the next morning's breakfast . . .

Another recipe, this time for a preventive rather than a cure, "has been tested and found successful for ages," according to a letter I read once from a man in Pakistan. He was adding his bit to a lengthy discussion about birth control which was going on in the correspondence columns of an international weekly, and he did it in such a toplofty way, with such cocksure superiority, that it is impossible not to print most of what he wrote:

"I read with great interest and contempt the futile efforts of your so-called great doctors to discover a certain method for not having babies, besides abstention, that is. May I offer a sure and much-tested way? If a woman catches a frog and, after spitting thrice in its face, leaves it where she found it, she will not be pregnant again."

Then, after assuring the editor of the magazine that the success of this remedy is age-old, the writer conceded, "Some people may laugh at this suggestion."

I do not. I do not laugh at any medical folklore. But I wish that I knew the belief behind the act, the spiritual dependence upon a certain legend that would make a wary woman pick up a frog rather than an egg, or spit in that poor staring face rather than a rat's or a spider's.

Between the toad and the dove there is more than mere space. One hops in the mud and dust, and croaks its love song in a parody of the soft coo or the shrill insistent plaining of the varied birds we call pigeons. They in turn fly easily in another element, and light at will upon the highest spires.

Mostly we ignore the first, and use the latter agelessly in poetry, as well as gastronomically in the kitchen pot.

Pigeon broths, perhaps because the birds are so often sung about by lovesick bards, have been a restorative for centuries after the various fatigues and enervations of amorous pursuit, and have even been served in pies and puddings to do the opposite and spur it on.

The receipt I like the best, divorced from such venery and as straightforward as cruel innocence itself, was told me by Nigel, in Mexico. He said that once he met his laundress coming up from the lake, where she had been washing, with a huge basket of clothes on her head and one of her little sons dragging along behind her. She held a live pigeon firmly in her hand.

"The boy's got a little fever," she said. "I'm going to put him into bed, and then I'll split open this pigeon and lay it on his stomach."

What Nigel told about the poor bird and what Georges taught me when he called his little son a toad, all came into focus one day much later in Provence, so that I felt no real astonishment and only a kind of identification with the ancient shapes and forms of the world about me. It was a good experience.

I was standing with two small children at the roadside in a hamlet where the bus went through only twice a week. There were two or three Algerians huddled apart from the old peasant women waiting with us. We would all go into Aix, do our various errands, and come home our own ways, to separate until the next bus, divided by race and various other less obvious barriers. But in the sun, with the cigales shrilling, we could talk as if we had long known one another, and when one old woman with a basket of eggs for the market suddenly clutched at me and cried, "No no! Tell them to be careful, to be kind!" I was not at all startled, but called out automatically to the two little girls who were ambling across the road.

"Come back," I said.

They looked up curiously at me and said, "But there is the most *beautiful* toad here!"

The old woman sighed and let go of me.

"Oh, they are good children," she said. "Sometimes little people are mean to toads. These girls are all right. But the toads are my friends, my real friends, not people. People are bad."

She was not much more than half my height, and she was without any teeth at all, but through her mumblings I could understand the words, and in her small ancient eyes I could read the truth: she was not mad, not even tetched. When she asked, "Do you want to know why toads are more my friends than people?" I bent down to hear, with all my inner and outer ears listening, and beckoned silently to the little girls to come and listen too.

When the old woman was a little girl, she told us, she had died. She lay for two days lifeless on the bed where she had succumbed to typhoid fever, like so many other villagers of those far days, and her family slept on the floor, and everyone came in and sprinkled holy water on her from the bowl of it by the door and then sat weeping and drinking in the other room, the kitchen.

The priest came for the last time: she was to be buried the next day. When he had left, her mother cried "No, no!" and she ran out with a pillowcase in her hand. She had gone off her head, people said pityingly.

But she came back, and in the pillowcase were a dozen toads, trying clumsily to hop against the thick cloth, and in her hand was a live pigeon.

Perhaps with the priest safely out of the way it was easier to go about the next step, which the villagers now knew the mother was about to do. She tied the mouth of the pillowcase firmly, and put it all hopping and thumping in the bottom of the funeral bed, at the feet of the little body. Then she split the live pigeon and clapped it upon her dead child's head, where the warm gushing blood ran down over the chilled skin and where, most probably, the bird's heart still beat a few more times in its halved shell of feathers.

I can imagine that some of the neighbors kept watch

all night, partly from Christian custom and partly to pray for the ancient magic to work. Certainly the ones who saw the child begin to breathe softly are now dead, for the old woman who told us of this was herself ancient by the time we met at the bus stop. But she had not lost her sense of wonderment, and she clutched my arm again fiercely as she looked up at me and asked, "Am I not right to call the toad my friend? Am I not right to protect him from all the cruel stupid people who tease him and kick him? Toads live forever. It may be that very one there in the road that warmed my feet when I died."

She said abruptly to me, "Watch my egg basket," and then she took the two little girls by the hand and together they went out into the hot road where the enormous toad sat panting. She picked it up carefully, much as a young mother lifts a new wet baby from its bath, and on the opposite side of the road she put it down and the three of them pushed a little dust close around it.

The other people from her village did not seem to notice all this, as if they were used to it, but from the shade I could see the Algerian women watching brightly, and I wondered if they perhaps could remember a like happening.

Then the bus came down the road, and the old peasant and the children ran back.

"See?" she asked me triumphantly. "We saved it again. The bus would have crushed it flat, maybe."

We climbed aboard. I handed up the basket of eggs. Nothing more happened until we got out, in Aix, and then before she headed for the market place she hurried to us and said, "Come to my cabin whenever you wish, and I'll give you each a fresh egg."

And now whenever I think of toads, or see one, I think of her and see the glaring road in the little village, with the silent Algerian women, the silent villagers, one toothless small old peasant, and her friend, the great dust-colored silent toad.

I think of pigeons too, but not in the same way. Perhaps it is because the pigeon that died for her was once and for all dead, whereas the sackful of toads hopped away from the death chamber, their duty done.

VII

What is man, when you come to think
upon him, but a minutely set,
ingenious machine for turning, with
infinite artfulness, the red wine of
Shiraz into urine?

Isak Dinesen

Just as new words come into a language steadily, especially after wars and occupations, so old words dwindle
and then grow again, in both usage and meaning. I can
think of dozens of current ones that I did not know at all
when I was young, like radar and cyclotron and vitamin,
and of several which as I came to know them I also knew
never to say, or only to whisper. Some were said by
grownups, but they too whispered them, or chose their
listeners with finicky caution.

I remember being only faintly amused when my most
worldly uncle confessed at teatime to my mother that he
had been "somewhat taken aback" to be told, that morning, that one of their mutual friends was expecting. Her
condition was not what shocked him, but rather the fact

that the word "pregnant" had been *used on the street,* and by an *unmarried woman.* Such a thing would never have occurred a few years before, he said, and I could sense that he was thankful I, a virginal eighteen or so, had not been with him when it did.

Maybe a year later I paid the price for my advanced feeling that a few such barriers should be hurdled overtly, and was informed on paper not to read aloud before the class, as was the firm custom, my winning essay in which I had written, not once but twice, the same word that had disturbed my uncle.

The odd thing there was that I had not even referred to a female animal, but to a clause in the Constitution, which in my youthful way I felt was "pregnant with meaning."

My professor's prudery was not as much of a shock to me, however, as was the last time I was sent from the dining table by my father.

I was perhaps sixteen, but I felt myself a mature woman of the world, which of course subjected me to unusual scrutiny by my parents as I tried out various new mannerisms and affectations in my search for what I really might be. That is undoubtedly why my father was unfair to me. He thought I was deliberately trying to be coarse and vulgar when I in complete innocence remarked that something was about the size of a rabbit turd.

I was astonished by glacial silence, and when my father asked me quietly to leave the room I stumbled out in a state of bewildered embarrassment.

Later I told him that I had spoken without any

thought of trying to shock, and that I did not know the word was forbidden. True, I had never heard it spoken anywhere but in the Back Yard.

"Precisely," he said.

By now, I think it has risen from the barnyard to the parlor (if not the dining room), rather as gin has come up from the lowest London grogshop to the palace. Turd and dung are all right in their ever-widening places, although some other euphemisms for fecal excrement are still classed as definitely "four-letter words," like most of the ones for urine.

I know of some strange receipts which contain these two materials, the liquid and the solid, which all animal bodies must make and then excrete in order to exist. They are very old, I am sure, and although some of them are still used, it is mostly by very simple or isolated people who have to depend upon instinctive chemical knowledge for their remedies, instead of buying elaborately disguised copies of them from modern laboratories.

I think the first time I ever saw that urine was saved and used was when my mother whispered to me that mixed with an equal part of water it would make smilax ferns grow long and beautiful.

She shuddered a little when she confided this to me, and I wished that like many others of the respectable houses in Whittier, ours could have two large hanging baskets of the strangely nourished plants on the front porch. It was because of Mother, I thought regretfully; she was too dainty . . .

Surely it was not from her, then, that I heard, also in

whispers, that Southern girls had the whitest skins in America because they patted themselves each night with their own warm urine, perfumed with lavender?

This clashed, colorwise at least, with a later bit of knowledge told me by a Negro in Delaware, that all her boys were the handsomest family in the country and got the most girls, because their skins were the softest. From boyhood, she said proudly, they had rubbed themselves at courting time with their pee-juice.

It will cure freckles, too, according to a woman I knew on a farm in Provence.

She suffered mightily from them when she was a teasable child, until her grandmother, who was mountain-born, gave her this recipe:

Take a wineglass of urine and mix it with a tablespoon of good vinegar. Add a pinch of salt. Let it sit for 24 hours. Then pat it on the freckled skin and leave it for one half-hour, and rinse off with plain cold water.

This recipe is also good for freshening the skin of people who have been ill or who crave more beauty, she added . . . which I suppose would let it qualify for both the colored boys in Delaware and the lily-white Southern girls?

I have not heard of any recipes for internal medication with urine, but an Irishman did tell me one remedy for severe insect stings which used it. You must move fast, he said; scoop up a handful of dry dust, pee into it, and mold it quickly into a plaster, and slap it onto the stung place, to prevent any pain at all, or swelling.

I don't know about this from my own experience, but it has a dramatic earthiness to it.

Dung, now, at least from animals, is more often used both inwardly and outwardly, and I have a few odd recipes in proof of it.

For instance there is one which I first heard from a hired girl we had in Whittier. She was from a farm in Kansas, a runaway to the ever-brightening lights of Hollywood.

She must have been fairly free-spoken for those days, because it was after she had explained in some detail to me what the word "rape" meant that she left us hurriedly, and I was told to forget *everything* she may have said.

My parents did not suspect that a statutory offense interested me much less in those golden days than did a folk recipe, and that her panacea for breaking a fever still stays in my mind. (This is partly because I have heard several other people repeat it in much the same form.)

She was a pretty girl, still nursing the baby that was the result of her four-letter sexual experience, and she loved to talk to me over the sweet little nuzzling body in her wretched "maid's room," after dinner was cleared away.

She was fascinating to me because she took much simple pleasure in describing things at length which were never mentioned in my family, although plainly they were going on all around us. She could tell wonderfully detailed stories about dying, for instance: various odors, various noises that were made, various ways corpses looked. And among other things I learned from her, using a word which once cost me my dinner, is this receipt:

To Break a Fever, as in Measles

Gather plenty of turds from the wild jackrabbit, and dry them in the oven to keep for the winter in a jar. When a fever will not break, make a very strong tea of the dung and hot water, strain it, and drink it every half-hour until the sweating starts. This never fails.

Wild jackrabbits do not lope over the Kansas prairies as they used to, but from what I have heard, country people still use much this same remedy, made from the neat droppings of their barnyard substitutes, and a friend from Australia swears that he has been given kangaroo tea for fever. Kangaroos are of the same family, I think?

Here is a receipt collected by Ann Blencowe in Elizabethan England which has some faint and fancified resemblance to this plain tea, but using manure:

To make ye horse dunge water, for Agues and feavers and all distempers. Take horse dunge and putt to it so much Ale as will make it like hasty puding, and put it into your still. Then putt on ye topp one pound of treakell, and a quarter of a pound of genger in powder and the same in sweet anisseeds, and so distill all these together. This water also is good for women in labor and in childbed.

A potion made of some of the same ingredients, but to my rather hesitant palate much pleasanter to think of taking, is from the same *Receipt Book of Ann Blencowe*:

Plurecy Water, Likewise good
for Grip & Fitts in Children

Take of Stone Horse Dunge new Made 8 Pound, Annisseeds brused & licquorish sliced, of Each two ounces, Raisins of the sun stoned 2 Ounces, & Venus Treacle one ounce. Put all these into 3 quarts of strong White wine: stir it well together & cover it & let it stand by the fire all night. The next Day still it in a Cold Still.

These recipes could as well, I suppose, be classed among the herbs as here, for they are based on digested grasses and leaves of the vegetarian animals, which have of course undergone some natural fermentation in the intestines and have thus kept much of their bacillic action.

All this intuitive use of acids and protective healing elements reminds me of the one recipe I have heard in which, even indirectly, human excrement is used. It was told to me by the friend who was raised far in the hidden part of Brazil.

He said that for coughs and fevers, the village women would brew a kind of infusion made from the oldest and most soiled mattress they could find, usually a child's. They would take out some of the cornhusks it was stuffed with, pound them in a mortar, and then pour river water over the fruity powder. If it did not seem strong enough of the old human leavings they were relying upon, they would get a little boy to pee into the bowl, just a few more drops.

This would of course stop a cough or fever or almost *anything,* my friend said with a shudder of recently acquired gentility.

VIII

To blow and swallow at the same
moment is not easy.

Plautus

A poet once wrote to me from a ship bound toward New
York from Bremen, "I would drink more than I do if I
were not out of ship's money. A few dollars are left, it's
true, and therefore I shall drink anyway. The stupendous
virtue of drink! I feel fat when I drink, fat and snuffy as a
porpoise. The truth is I have my annual cold and feel
cosmic."

The involutions of this are countless. He felt snuffy as
a porpoise because he had a cold, not because of the
drink, and he felt cosmic because of the drink, not because of the cold, and so on and on. He was, no matter
what his outline of the affair, supremely lucky that, having a cold, he also had something to drink, for as far as I

know there is nothing more comforting in this world, on land or sea, than grog for human fog.

A cold of any type but especially the kind accepted fatalistically as "annual" by most people is one of the great psychological ignominies of modern life. Its humiliations, too well known to recount, are endless and depthless. Its prevention and cure are equally questionable, but most of the pleasanter suggestions for them deal, more often than not, with alcohol.

I have met a few people who seemed impervious to cold infection, and without exception they were moderate but seasoned whiskey drinkers. This, to my mind, is more than coincidence. I believe firmly that their judicious intake of alcohol kept them, in a fairly obvious way, as aseptic as a hospital thermometer standing in its solution (although of course thermometers do not have livers to grow cirrhotic or at least maimed by the liquor).

One of the first little jokes I learned when I went to live in France was a kind of proverb:

How to Cure a Cold

One tall silk hat, one four-poster bed, one bottle of brandy. To be taken as follows: put the tall silk hat on the right-hand post at the foot of the bed, lie down and arrange yourself comfortably, drink the brandy, and when you see a tall silk hat on both the right and *left* bedposts you are cured.

This may be a somewhat Gallic exaggeration, but it is based on sound sense, and in the face of my grandmother's teetotaling ghost I repeat with complete con-

fidence that the least harmful and most comforting medicine for any average human being laid low with his "annual cold" is what my poet friend called, bluntly, drink.

Even without the added lull of liquor, though, a long
hot drink, and a modicum of peace and quiet, can do
more to soften the misery of a rheumy bout than anything else yet evolved by man, and this next family remedy has comforted both old and young for generations,
after its fashion, although it was written for children:

> Sit well wrapped in a blanket with your feet in a basin of
> water which is kept very hot, for one half-hour, and sip
> slowly at a mug kept filled with lemonade made with fresh
> lemon juice, plenty of sugar or honey, and boiling water.
> Then get into bed.

The sense of this is plain, for modern doctors, even
with antibiotics and other "miracle drugs" at their
command, still say that plenty of liquid plus plenty of
rest are the best remedies for the Common Cold (Sir William Osler, one of the world's great doctors, prescribed
somewhat the same thing: No food, bed rest, and a good
book . . .), and I have yet to know a human being who
will not respond almost voluptuously, no matter how
wretched he may feel, to the enforced repose of a hot foot
bath, his innards awash with the tonic impact of lemon
and honey.

Even if he must race at the end of the half-hour to a
board meeting instead of bed, he will feel better than before, less like a snuffy porpoise.

Snuffiness alone, even without all the other horrid

symptoms, is almost enough to make anyone regret his natal day. Fortunately there are pocket inhalers now, so that a man can take a couple of good drags occasionally of the volatile oils of menthol and eucalyptus and various other harmless specifics.

Relief of this kind is temporary but harmless, when sought with any good sense, and I can still remember the sharp pleasure I felt when I was a child and my mother would let me put a touch of mentholatum up my nostrils. The first deep sniff was almost painful, and then all too soon I wanted more of the patented balm that was one of our rare family panaceas. It was rationed, for some reason, as if it were nine-tenths opium or perhaps attar of roses, which in turn added to my pleasure, of course. I had to wait until I was obviously miserable again for the next happy inhalation.

An even simpler version of this help, which was undoubtedly common long before it was noted in 1650 in a pharmacist's book, is the following:

For a Cold in ye head, take sage leaves, rub them well, and apply them to ye nostrils in ye morning.

Vicarious suffering can be even more acute than actual, with colds as with other less tangible ills, and school-teachers have told me that there is only one thing more exhausting than a roomful of snuffling pupils, and that is one in the next step of this epidemic ordeal, the coughing. Some of them even swear that children *love* to cough, especially in unison, and especially if they can manage to reduce their schoolmistresses to screams or tears.

My mother never taught school, but she has told me that she almost went mad with only two children at the coughing stage one long dank winter in Ventura on the California coast. She was alone with my sister and me in a big ill-heated house just beyond the high-tide line, and according to apocryphal reports we coughed steadily and loudly, like seals, through every remedy she tried on us, until finally she simply sat in the din with tears running down.

Then a Mexican neighbor came in shyly, with a little pitcher full of what became a standard prescription for us and our own children and many others:

> Equal parts of honey, glycerine, and fresh lemon juice, mixed well, to be eaten with a spoon and let slide down the throat slowly . . .

Another cough remedy, which my mother scoffed at, partly because it was told to us by a woman who had temporarily supplanted her in our affections, was a pale and eminently ugly pastille called slippery elm drops, to be dissolved slowly in the mouth.

I can agree now with my mother that these flat pills were slimy, but during one of her absences they were showered upon my sister and me by a tall godlike woman who acted as nanny-substitute, and who read *Hiawatha* by the hour while my little sister and I combed out her extraordinarily long and beautiful auburn hair. This goddess was up to no good, I later learned, and soon after her stay with us ran off with another protégé of my grandmother, who had hired her. (Both the girl and her swain, who was conveniently boarding next door, became missionaries, which took the curse off their promiscuity at least.)

I shall always remember her endless supply of slippery elm, and the way my mother got cross when we asked for it, and the long gleaming hair. "By the shore of Gitche Gumee / By the shining Big-Sea-Water . . ." and the saliva rushes to my mouth and slips smoothly down and the cough drowns.

A good remedy noted in Ann Blencowe's *Receipt Book* is called:

The Gargle for Mrs. Barnardiston

Take one handfull Rasp Berry leaves, and put to it a pint of water boil'd down to a quarter of a pint. Add to it one Table spoonfull of Honey & two Tea spoonfulls of Lemon Juice.

This is of course like the Ventura syrup. I do not know how the infusion of raspberry leaves replaces the glycerine, nor do I know if there is the same soothing quality in them as there might be in the pure juices of the fruit, but I can state that black currants in place of raspberries have helped many a hacking miserable human.

The first time I proved it was during a bleak winter in Dijon, when I had reached the noisiest part of what some people would call resignedly "my annual cold." I was in one of the last of the provincial music halls, the "caf'-con," where people sat at round tables and watched on a small stage an evening of vaudeville acts which ranged from terrible to middling to occasionally great. Apparently I coughed so unconcernedly and loudly, having grown used to myself, that the management felt obliged to protect the actors and the audience, and a small glass of the local black currant cordial called *cassis* was put silently alongside my coffee. The waitress whispered to me to sip it when I felt a tickling in my throat. I did. It worked. Since then I have felt a real respect for it, in every form from the white wine laced with it which the Dijonnais call for the moment (I cannot bring myself in this case to write "currently," which is the correct word, no matter how spelled) a Kir, in honor of their fantastic old Mayor, and on to the Black Currant Pastilles which are made in England and are almost as slippery and juice-making as the elm drops of my childhood.

Pastilles are at least a little sweetened, perhaps to cajole us into eating more, but in parts of France a remedy is brewed which has no cajolery in it, and is for the stalwarts among sufferers. It is to be used as a gargle, for sore throats, and it is a strong tea made of the dried leaves and flowers of wild blackberries, the kind that grow in the hedges along country roads. It whips and scours like nettles, I am told, and then the rasp is gone with the sting.

Probably even such a gargle, even such a gastronomical insult as a pastille, can be classified as "cuisine," and surely the hot onion soups that many Europeans have prescribed to me for colds (as well as hang-overs) spring originally from man's undying appetite. These soups are in the main delicious, and like anything potable which is even indirectly connected with the cure of our universal

nd nights to as many thousands, and his voice be-
ow and then a squeak rather than a mighty roar.
led his fatigue "bronchial," and this is what he ad-

e Taken When Leaving
rm Room for the Cold

lve in a half-glass of very cold vinegar about a spoonful
and half as much of cayenne pepper. Warm and let
gain.

ood preacher possibly, indeed probably, felt that
ly hot potion would protect him from the icy air
iries without benefit of liquor, of which he was
but his nostrum is almost sacrilegiously like
ree others I have heard, which used straight
nd plain pepper or pepper sauce, and left out
s the barmen once used to say, "Choose your
"
has apparently long been a comforter to the
dy when it is besogged with all the evil ele-
Cold. One cure I remember, this time for the
that so often presages wheezier if less actively
es to come, is to boil ground black pepper
gether, and then inhale their fumes. This is
pt, and still used in the Kentucky moun-
England originally, I suspect.
this time told me by a man from Vermont,
esh spruce leaves or gum. This will cure a
one day, he assured me. I suppose, hopeful-
far from spruce trees, that syrups and pas-

malady, they are most efficacious when drunk in a warm
bed. They range from the delicate to the robust.

A Delicate Onion Soup

　　1 large mild onion
　　1 tablespoon butter
　　1 cup milk, hot but not boiling

Peel and slice very thin the onion, into a pan where the
melted butter will wilt it without browning. Add the hot
milk, and strain. Serve at once in a bowl or cup.

A Robust Onion Soup

　　1 large or 2 small onions
　　1 tablespoon butter
　　1 cup strong broth

Slice the peeled onion and brown in the butter. Add the
broth, and simmer until the onion is soft. Serve unstrained.

The most rugged experience I ever had with an onion
was for a cold cure, and like most such prescriptions it
was made with compassion and in this case with love
too.

I was young and completely catarrhal, in a dank town
where I longed to be warm, glamorously mature, and
unhampered by the wheezings and snuffles of an abys-
mally humiliating cold. Fortunately my husband shared
my wishes, and after a short time of considering me cool-
ly, in terms of social desirability at least, he told me of an
infallible remedy for what ailed me.

"Eat this onion," he said, after a quick trip to the
market. "It is a strong one, but don't hesitate. Bite right

into it as if it were a good apple, and chew it up and swallow it. It may make your eyes water a little, but that is just the way it should be. Gets rid of the poisons. Wonderful stuff really."

Love as well as despair blinded me before the tears did, of course, and I still hope they all acted as a kind of anesthetic for the wild blasting of my senses that followed my first resolute bite. I was on fire. I was in Hell. From the shoulders up to the last hair on my head I buzzed like an agonized bee in every atom of my skin and flesh and bone. When I gasped, my husband whacked me and said, "Good, good. That's the way it should be. Clearing you out. Killing the germs. Excellent reaction. You'll be fine before you know it."

I was not, and spent three days in bed with severe blisters in my mouth and throat, but the cold was gone. It had been routed. It is almost literally the last one I have ever had, just as that onion is the last one I have eaten raw for a cold cure since 1929, when the stock market and I crashed.

Another remedy which sounds somewhat messier to prepare, if not actually impossible, is more fun to ponder on. It comes from a Canadian collection of household recipes of every sort, from the buttery to the "phisical receipts," and it probably reached the Dominion from some battered Elizabethan daybook. It is called "Mrs. Margaret Burton's Plaster."

It is a stiff hot mixture of beeswax, resin, and oil of mace melted together and then spread upon the fleshy

side of a piece of fresh leather, pre
This would of course be hard to fi
nadian farm, but if by chance it
moment, care should be taken
shape, large enough to be laid
upon the Breast, pritty high, &
stomach.

"It must not be held by the
tinue, "but laid on & with the
one side. 'Twill make it stick.
off Lay on another, & keep th
done great cures."

Here again, in coping wi
heat and, above all, rest, fo
dash about with a large
sheep's leather on his front?
it were pressed there by "th
one who loved him?

Some people cough mo
quite often have trouble
like my Cockney friend
He lived to a ripe age o
cines, mostly alcoholic,
the most, a preventive
the *Autobiography* of P
odist preacher.

He rode the circui
days when a man cou
in a lonely cabin, or

days
came
He ca
vised:

To
a W

Diss
of sal
chill

The g
this wil
of the pr
arch foe,
two or t
whiskey
the salt.
poison . .

Pepper
human bo
ments of a
sore throat
painful tin
and milk t
an old rece
tains—from

Another,
is to chew f
sore throat i
ly, since I an

tilles containing some product of spruce or balsam or even hemlock trees would help . . . or perhaps liberal drafts of spruce beer? I assume that this is somewhat headier than a mere tea, and would therefore be able to add a mild alcoholic blessing to the self-medication.

Or why dot siblify everythig ad drig a grog?

IX

Misery treads on the heels of joy;
anguish rides swift after pleasure.
Donald Grant Mitchell

Sometimes it is impossible to tell when a preventive is only that and not a cure as well, for ailing man or beast. This is not the case with hang-overs, at least.

There is one and only one positive and infallible preventive for this ancient and universal physical hazard: abstention.

Its cures, most of them of small value but enormous social interest, are almost as many as there are people to invent them. They cover every conceivable procedure, and range from the somber to the silly. One man who spent much of his lifetime studying the problem through his own reactions to it insisted, long before he was knocked down and killed when cold sober by an enormous dog, that the only real cure was sudden death. This assertion was even more macabre to his friends because he had always professed, and backed it by practice, that two aspirins and "a hair of the dog that had bit him" were of great help the morning after the night before . . .

It is interesting that most hang-over cures seem to involve more alcohol, even indirectly, as in a peculiar one still used occasionally in sporting circles. It is at least as old as *The Beggar's Opera,* and from the same social level as Macheath and Suky Tawdry.

It evolved, probably, from the basic fact that most black eyes are suffered by brawlers too drunk to duck, and that a basic cure for black eyes in those rough days, as even now, was to bleed them with leeches.

Leeches are, however, capable of being surprisingly fastidious, and most of them do not like alcohol in their drink. Occasionally one turns up, however, which loves booze as fiercely as any habitual tosspot, and which will suck from his fellow drunkard until he is, leech-wise, roaring.

Naturally such alcoholic jewels are rare, and when once found in the circles that most need them, in tough London a few centuries ago and in tough New York in 1890, they have been handed tenderly from one "physician" to another until, I assume, they have died an alcoholic death.

It is difficult to imagine how to tell a drunken leech from a sober one, and I feel willing to let the whole peculiar question rest on hearsay, in this case from a well-read old man who had tried to earn his way through medical college and ended as a rubber in a rundown gymnasium for pugilists.

It is a relief to come upon a nonalcoholic remedy for a hang-over, and here is one as innocent as a new-born butterfly. It was given to me by a devout and therefore teetotaling Methodist, who recommended it from her own experience for fatigue or an upset stomach, but confessed that her pop, before he Heard the Call, often ate great quantities of it after his weekly trips into town from the Kansas farm:

Buttermilk [for?] Pop

Mix one tablespoonful of cornstarch in one cup of good buttermilk, and heat but do not boil. Eat while hot like soup, with salt and pepper, or let cool and eat frequently, with plenty of honey for flavoring.

I have tried this, not from necessity but from curiosity, and cold it is a pleasantly refreshing bowl, somewhat like yoghurt. I can imagine that it would prove a balm to the outraged innards of anyone who had drunk too much, or suffered from some other kind of poisoning.

I asked my friend from Kansas why she put "plenty of honey" in the recipe she copied for me from her old book, and she did not rightly know, but reminded me that "honey never hurt *any*body." This may not be completely so, but a current vogue for curing hang-overs with large regulated doses of it would bear her out in that it never hurt an otherwise healthy drunkard.

According to a Vermont doctor who has observed local

folk medicine for a long time and written successfully about some of his simple conclusions, overindulgence in hard liquor is caused by a lack of potassium in the human system. Honey, he says, is one of the best natural supplies of this alkaline, and will not only soothe a body drowned in alcoholic acids but will help kill a craving for them.

Vermonters, especially as interpreted by scientists, are practical, hard-headed people. Those of us who are less so may prefer to think that an urge to go on a spree is more the fault of a faithless lover or a carefree friend than of a potassium deficiency, but no matter what the cause of a night or even a week of sousing, two pounds of honey and twenty-four hours of rest are almost a sure cure, not only for the temporary ungodliness of the hang-over but for the first desire, too.

Dr. Jarvis's Honey Cure

18 teaspoonfuls of honey, to be given 6 at a time, 20 minutes apart. Then repeat in 3 hours. Let patient drink whiskey left by bed if he wishes. Next morning repeat 40-minute honey-routine, follow with soft-boiled egg, and then in 10 minutes give 6 more teaspoonsful of honey. For lunch give 4 t. honey, then glass of tomato juice, medium piece of chopped beef, and for dessert 4 more t. honey. Leave whiskey on table toward normal evening meal, but it will probably not be drunk.

I have never known anyone to follow this cure for such a serious hang-over as the one reported in the book about Vermont folk medicine, when the patient had been drinking for some two weeks and was "paralyzed drunk" (although apparently still able to swallow!) when the honey treatment began. But I know several people who have sobered themselves by sipping honey and milk, preferably in a dark quiet room, for a few hours after they or their protective friends have realized that alcohol was in command. Even without regarding the fine word potassium, their bodies have recognized the need to counteract the acids gnawing at them, and like animals or children they have welcomed the sweet balm.

X

Put not your trust in vinegar . . .
Eugene Field

Alcohols have long been used in a more positive medical way than to cure the poor souls who have abused them, with or without the aid of honey, and even leeches. Since they emerged from the alchemists' crucibles of the Middle Ages as *aqua vitae,* on down to some such quackish advertisement as this one clipped from an American newspaper circa 1880, they have been leaned upon by ailing man:

> Buy Cobham's, No Other! Your physician will tell you that you should always have some good whiskey in the house! For accidents, fainting spells, exhaustion, and other emergency cases, it relieves and revives. But you must have GOOD whiskey, *pure* whiskey, for poor adulterated whiskey may do decided harm. *Buy Cobham's!!!*

Nothing is said in this enthusiastic blurb about the method of application, but from what I know about my country in those days, it was destined for internal use. Even at the quoted price of sixteen dollars for twenty quarts, prepaid, it would have been deemed a pity and an extravagance to waste it on a person's skin, as alcohols are still used in older civilizations.

The first time I knew that very old people, or ones who have been bedridden, could perhaps gain strength and even pleasure from the liquors that their families would rub them with, was when I lived in Switzerland.

Our vineyard had a pretty fruit orchard in its little meadow, and as soon as the cherries and then the plums and *mirabelles* and finally the pears and apples began to drop from their trees, we would pick them up and toss them into several large barrels set out for them. Wasps and midges got drunk on the gases from them and the rotten juice, and though it was pleasant to rummage in the grass each night before dark, and then again in the cool mornings, I could not see how the dirty mess in the barrels would ever change into a decent thing to drink.

Finally it was hauled off to the community distiller, and heavily taxed as I remember, and when the one-liter bottles came back for our cellar, they were filled with what looked like vile colorless firewater, marked *Cherry, Mirabelle,* and so on, with the date and the alcoholic percentage.

"This dozen is for five years from now, or later, to be drunk for festivals," I was told. "These twenty bottles we will mark for year after next, to be tasted and perhaps blended with some older stuff. And these here, because the quality is so high this year, are for frictions and massage. They are wonderful. Here, try some of the *kirschwasser* . . ."

A little was rubbed on my arm, and I could feel the warmth go through my whole body, and most miraculous, I could feel on my pinkened skin the *spirit* of the fruit, the taste-smell-feel of a fine ripe cherry.

In the next short years there, we gave several bottles of our unadorned elixir to people who were unwell, aching, feverish—both young and ancient. One of them was an old woman with a protracted pneumonia who had often been kind to me. She said our alcohol was the best to cleanse and purify that she had ever felt. And once I strained an ankle badly, and rubbings with an alcohol of our rotted pears kept the swelling down, the flesh healthy, and me happier on my couch.

Before we left, we were able to drink some too, and it was a good, straight gut-reaching potion which would lose its roughness before much longer. It was like a crude *marc,* without the taste of grape. It made a decent grog, with hot water and lemon and honey, for weariness or a cold or the misery.

The nearest thing in our country to this European use of good alcohol, to reduce swellings and fevers and to keep things fresh and sterile in the sickroom, is cider vinegar, used everywhere apples grow in America.

My own grandfather used it on his lame shoulders like a liniment, and on his saddle horses too, and I am sure he would bear me out that it has long served as a liquid and in poultices for burns, insect bites, and rashes. When I was a little girl it was added to the rinse water for my hair, to burnish it like a pony's coat.

More seriously, New Englanders believe that its application with gentle rubbing will do much to help if not actually cure arthritis, rheumatism, and even varicose veins in man and beast. How much of this comes from the soothing warmth of the massage, and how much from the various elements of the fermented apple juice, I cannot say. I do know that part of my pleasure in my grandfather's "clean" smell came from the good apple cider vinegar on his skin . . .

XI

Purge me with hyssop, and I shall be
clean: wash me, and I shall be whiter
than snow.

Psalm 51:7

Cider vinegar and water, spiked with a little honey, has
long been recognized as a good cleanser of a tired or
abused digestive system. (I do not know that it has any
purgative qualities, although like most half-fermented
fruit juices fresh cider will act as a "physic" if one drinks
too much of it at a Hallowe'en party.)

Diuretics are a dime a dozen in any folk medicine, and
where a man in Vermont must depend upon his apple
orchard, and a European upon his white wine grapes,
Mexican peasants near Guadalajara will drink floods of
tea made from boiled grasshopper legs and get the same
relief. All this seems to indicate that liquid itself, rather
than what is in it, is the thing that best and most logical-
ly stirs up a sluggish liver!

Folk medicine can adjust itself smoothly to the current fashion, and where purges were once given for every phase and form of that almost obligatory gentlemen's disease, the Gout, now Hepatitis steals the show, whether it be chronic, mild, acute, infectious.

As has long been the case, cures based on vegetable oils and extracts seem to assuage more sufferers with less direful aftereffects than do the "miracle drugs," and good old castor oil, the bane of my childhood, starts out at least three cures I have heard about lately from friends in Paris.

One of them was told to me with drama in every syllable by a beautiful blonde creature whose solid reputation in the French theater depends at least a little on the equal solidity of a liver affronted continuously by the dietetic obligations of keeping that reputation solid. It is hard to be ascetic socially when "everyone" seems to live on Scotch and smoked salmon, with champagne and caviar as a somewhat outmoded but still acceptable substitute. My beautiful friend found herself facing her next season with a fat fine part in a sure hit, and the bitter yellowish feeling in her soul which only an outraged liver can impose.

Her "three-day cure," stripped of the artful huggermuggery which can make even a glass of plain water vitally amusing and delicious, especially to people of the Theater, consisted of what my mother would have called "a good course of the sprouts," and what a Harley Street baronet once taught me to refer to as a "tail-raiser"—a thorough physicking. In this case the key action induced by castor oil was preceded and then followed by the gentler, more smoothing, effects of pure olive oil, in carefully timed doses interspersed with teas and more stimulating cordials made from many pleasant-tasting herbs.

Anyone who has taken even an average dose of castor oil knows that it is not exactly a restful experience, at least temporarily, but the actress told me that for three days she stayed in a quiet dim room dulled by the teas and cordials, and felt herself come to life and blossom like a sick houseplant which is given some sunlight and gentle rain.

Certainly she looked more beautiful than ever as, flourishing a smoked salmon canapé at me and sipping her Scotch, she told about it.

I have no idea what my mother's "course of sprouts" meant originally, or where she learned it, but I do know that it was her routine remedy for everything from a Bilious Attack to Plain Grumpiness (which she rightly ascribed to a sluggish interior). It consisted, until the day of my first declaration of independence, of a dose of castor oil stirred vigorously into a glass of fresh orange juice.

Now I loved oranges in every form, and not long after we moved to California, when I was four, I realized that Mother was in the process of ruining them for me forever. The thought of her pouring that oil into the delicious juice, and the thick sound I could hear in my head of the teaspoon hitting against the glass as it cut the globules of vile stuff into the liquid, and then the imagining of the sly ugly blending of the two flavors on my outraged palate: all made it plain that I must declare myself.

Of course this took reflection and planning, being the first such experience in my life. I talked my little sister into backing me up. I chose a time when my grandmother was away and my mother was rosy from a good solo she had sung in the choir.

I asked her straight if she would please never make me take castor oil again. I said, forging ahead fast so that she could not politely interrupt me, that I had learned from friends at school about other things like pills and even liquids, and that I would be glad to supply her with their names. I finished by telling her that I could not stand the thought of tasting castor oil even *one more time,* and that I would prefer to die first.

She obviously recognized my seriousness, and moved the bottle of oil from our upstairs bathroom to my grandmother's medicine closet on the ground floor, where it was apparently kept only for my mother's *accouchements* (to encourage labor!).

Somewhat unfortunately I neglected, in my nervousness, to tell her about the main objective, that I keep intact my enjoyment of the taste-smell-feel of oranges. My mother from then on used for her course of sprouts a bubbly bottled tail-raiser called Citrate of Magnesia, which fairly well disgusted me with the taste of lemonade for the rest of my life . . .

(My second formal declaration of independence, incidentally, hinged more on esthetics than on medical gastronomy, and came a few years later when I got my sister and the cook Elizabeth to witness and sign a paper stating that I would run away from home if my mother bobbed her hair. This was in 1920, perhaps, when Irene Castle's winsome derring-do had finally reached California . . .)

A purge I once read about, which most probably was based on castor oil, but which was much more artfully disguised and abetted than in my mother's receipt, was drunk by the high-living monks of an English abbey during the sixteenth century.

It was called A Drench, and was believed to be the least harmful of all the purges of that time to people who had steady recourse to it:

Take Milk and ye Oyl, a good pot. Put Aquavitae to it, and Peper and Brimstone, and mingle all Together. A pottle at a Time is not too much.

A spoonful, much less a pottle, would be enough for me, I think. I have never tasted Brimstone, even in the nursery medicine called sulfur and molasses in New England and brimstone and treacle in Old, but Milk and Peper are favorites of mine, and I would not have them risk the fate of my early taste for oranges. As for the Aquavitae, such is my faith in it that I doubt that even the other ingredients of this Drench could completely discourage me from drinking it, good brandy, in any form at all . . .

The only other thing with sulfur in it which I have copied for this peculiar hodgepodge of receipts is one I found in a Swiss herbal when I was looking for a way to make nettle soup . . . which is very good if the nettles are tender, and is exactly like a soup of spinach or water-cress, whether or not it is intended for a "spring tonic" as the winter-bound peasants most use it.

To Make a Poultice to Sooth the Pains of Rheumatism or any other: Pick stinging nettles and young oak leaves, chop them, put them into a fine handkerchief or piece of gauze, sprinkle them with sulfur, and bind firmly over the painful spot.

XII

Who hath not own'd, with rapture-
smitten frame,
The power of grace, the magic of a
name?

Thomas Campbell

One of the pleasantest things about writing all this is that the word *nettle* leads quirkily to *sulfur,* and then I can hop on to something as far removed as crab legs and crayfish tails, and from them to dreadful names like Asthma, Dropsy, Mad Dog, with almost all of them strung together on an invisible thread of growing plants-herbs-weeds ("A poisonous weed is a plant whose virtues have not yet been discovered," someone has said—perhaps Oliver Wendell Holmes).

Here, for instance, is what a woman in Mexico told me she always gave her children for a fever: twelve little crabs stewed in water. It was good for wheezings, too, she said. And here is an old English remedy for asthma, which certainly qualifies as a form of wheezing:

Dr. Nintle's Crawfish Broth
for Asthma and Swell'd Legs

Take half a pound of Lean Veal Cut in Slices, The Tails of Twelve live Crawfish with the Shell on them, Bruised in a Marble Mortar, three ounces of the root of Dandelion Bruised in a Marble Mortar. Put all this into a glazed Pipkin, with one Quart of Spring Water, & Let it boyl slowly over ye Coals intil it be reduced to one half. Put in half a handful of Watercress Chopt, and strain after one quarter hour and serve forth.

(This with a few minor changes, particularly about crushing live crayfish instead of freshly dead ones, and in marble instead of wood or even metal, makes a most delicious soup to be served without either asthma or dropsy as its excuse, like many other concoctions of the folk doctors.)

Another remedy for "swell'd legs," which seemed to be a fairly prevalent complaint in England some three hundred years ago, does not call for crayfish, and does not claim to cure anything but dropsy itself:

Lady Gage's Receipt

Take one Large Spoonfull every night & morning of unbruised mustard seed, drinking after each spoonfull ½ a pint of the following decoction.—Take 3 Large Handfulls of the Green top of Broom, boil them in one Gallon of water, keep Scumming of it. When there is no more scum take it off the fire & when cool pour it into an earthen vessel with the Broom. Of this decoction Lady Betty has continued taking ever since ye 23rd of June last, & will continue taking of it till Spring. Mustard seed is a great strengthen-ner of the Bowells, & Broom a Great Dieretick, so much as to fill a common chamber pot in 24 hours. The third day takeing the Medicine took away entirely her thirst. She is now neither swell'd in body nor Legs, no more than she was five years agoe. She is grown fatter & can walk an hour together without difficulty.

And here is another old prescription which, like Lady Gage's, is based on only one herb, used as much now as then. Her receipt called for the yellow-flowered broom which in pharmaceutical guise we now call scoparin; an Elizabethan physician used as an intrinsic part of his following cure not only our specific, liverwort, but the scheduled bathing which we now call hydrotherapy.

Dr. Meed's Certain Cure
for the Bite of a Mad Dog

Let the Patient be Blooded at the Arm, 8 or 10 Ounces. Take of the Herb Call'd in Latin Lichen Cinercus Terrestris, in English Ash Colour Liverwort, Clean dried & Powder'd, half an Ounce, of Black pepper two Drams. Mix these well together, & Divide the powder into 4 Doses, one of which must be taken every morning fasting, for 4 Mornings, Sussessively, in half a Pint of Cow's milk warm.

After these 4 Doses are taken, the Patient must go into the Cold Bath or Cold Spring or River every morning fasting for a month; he must be dipt all over, but not stay in with his Head above Water longer than half a Minute if the Water be very Cold; after this he must go in 3 times a week for a fortnight Longer. N.B. the Lichen is a very Common Herb, and grows generally in Sandy & Barren Soils all over England; the Right time to Gather it is in the Months of October and November.

Most old herbals and receipt books have at least one or two such "certain cures" for the bite of a mad dog in either man or beast, and it makes me wonder if perhaps the word "mad" meant simply infuriated in those days, and not "rabid" as it does for us. I have seen only two animals with rabies, but I have read that a man in the same condition is even more appalling. Certainly none of these sufferers could last the six and a half weeks of treatment prescribed by Dr. Meed, even with the magical simplicity of liverwort and cold river water!

Other illnesses, though, continue to respond to different waters, all over the world, just as they have for thousands of years.

The nicest hydrotherapy I know about, I think, was told to me by one of my own children, when she was little. She asked me with regret plain in her voice why she had never had an earache, and when I said something like I-don't-know-thank-God-but-why?, she told me that her dearest friend said it was the most fun in the world because of what her mother did to make it well: she had the little girl lie with her aching ear pressed against a pillow, and then on the other ear, the well one, she put steamy warm compresses for exactly one half-hour, while not a word was spoken and the clock ticked. My daughter told me of this yearningly, and I pondered on the gentle wisdom of it: the hypnotic half quiet, the warmth, the simplicity . . . above all, the trust in a wiser person's power.

Only lately I have heard of almost equally miraculous cures, of course bare of the mother-magic of this one, which are being worked in a suburb of Zurich by a self-styled doctor who submerges his patients in tubs of lukewarm water and then packs them with new-mown meadow grasses, mostly pink and white clover.

They emerge, I am told, feeling cleansed both inwardly and outwardly, and generally so refreshed that they are willing to sign statements swearing that they have been permanently cured of everything from "swell'd legs" and arthritis to a nagging wife.

This reminds me of another clover cure, which was solemnly recommended to me as a panacea for any form of cancer, but especially of the stomach or intestines: floods of tea made by steeping clover blossoms in hot water and adding a little honey.

The old carpenter who told me about this had cured himself, many years before, he said . . . and indeed when he died it was from a fall off a ladder, so perhaps he was right.

He is the man who showed me his bottle of Ozone once. He had bought it when a youngster from a traveling tent show, where the medicine man hung out charts of how active gangrene had been completely cured by a few applications of the Ozone. My friend said that with it he had saved the lives of several other carpenters with badly crushed fingers and blackening limbs.

I took a sniff of the grimy bottle, still half-full of a pale liquid in spite of its years of magic-making, and it did have a fresh stimulating smell, somewhat like good witch hazel.

"It has certainly lasted a long time, Mr. Addams," I said with no teasing visible.

He slipped it back into his hip pocket without a

smile, slapped it protectively, and said, "Yep. Wouldn't be here without it."

I could not tell whether he was paying tit for my tat, and left the room . . .

I have never seen gangrene cured by anything from a bottle, even when it is marked Ozone, but I am sure that I have often dosed myself with that on the desert below sea level, especially in May and in the moonlight, when the air seems filled with a pungent revivifying sting, and the fleeting perfumes of the tiny sand-flowers are almost visible. I have breathed so deeply of this double air as to feel drunk on it, so that the stars wheeled.

And I have never seen a man recover from a mad dog's bite, even when dosed with powdered liverwort. But I have seen a wart push itself out and away from a boy's hand because of a wort called, plainly enough, wart-wort.

This was interesting to watch. It happened a few summers ago, when a little boy called John came from California to stay on a farm in Provence with me. He arrived with several bottles which I could see had been very costly, and a habit of keeping one hand always in his pocket. He did indeed have the ugliest-looking wart I had ever seen, on the back of his right hand where it seemed to get hit with things, and to bang into them and rub against them. John said that he had used a dozen different medicines, and that if he had not had his ticket to Provence his mother would have arranged for an operation to remove this angry lump. Instead, he was supposed to dab on various things from the bottles, but they hurt and he kept forgetting. Meanwhile it grew worse, and I could see that he was humiliated as well as in some discomfort.

I told all this to a friend named Peter who lived in Aix and who knew so many strange things about other strange things—a kind of male Lolly Willowes really— that I thought he might well suggest something about John's burden.

"Of course," Peter said briskly. "Wartwort. Plain everyday old wartwort. We are walking right on it this minute."

And sure enough, the soft green carpet of June weeds, so soon to turn dry under the sun of the Provençal summer, was at least a third made up of this husky little plant. I do not know any other name for it, but I remember it from the hills of my childhood in the spring: of a tender green, fairly low to the ground but straggly, and with fragile juicy stems which when broken give out a drop or two of sticky white milk.

How I would have loved to know its impossibly silly name, when I was little! Now, even despairing John brightened at it, and when Peter told him the treatment he laughed with a mixture of doubt and delight and started it, right there on the path.

To Get Rid of a Wart in the Spring

Squeeze from the broken end of a wartwort stem the drop of milk, and dab it gently on the wart. Cover the whole wart, using as many stems of this limitless supply as you wish, but do not spread the milk past the edges of the wart. Do this three or four times a day for about two weeks. When the wart begins to push out of the healthy skin, take care not to joggle it and to push the wort milk gently under its loose edges. It will come off of itself, and then for a day or two put the wort milk on the place where it was, in case it left even a trace of its old tissue.

It was fine weather in Provence for the next two weeks, which meant that we ate outdoors and sat or walked or lay within arm's reach of John's remedy.

"Are you joking?" we had asked, and Peter had answered firmly, "You'll see," and we did, for the wart became almost a part of the family, not disgusting or humiliating at all, as we all picked the pretty weed and took turns touching its milk gently onto the intruder.

It changed every day, and once or twice at first it looked rather inflamed and rebellious and I got Peter to reassure me that I was doing no possible harm to indulge in this absorbing game. It began to grow out of the little crater it had made. In about ten days it was gone, one morning when John got up. He looked everywhere in his bed for it, because he wanted to keep it in a little matchbox he had found, to take back to California, but it never showed up.

I emptied the expensive bottles into the compost pit, feeling that plant decay would offset their noxious chemicals. It is possible that they contained exactly what hid in the pearly milk of the wartwort: I shall never know.

But when I look at John's smooth hand now, I remember what fun it was to rummage in the green weeds for the one we wanted, and then touch it so daintily to the ugly vanishing lump. Since that summer we have told a few people about it, but unless they are either from Provence or from very simple farm stock they do not really believe us.

XIII

Qu'a de saivi dins soun jardin
A pas besoun de médecin.
(Sage in the garden?
No need for Sawbones!)
                              Provençal Proverb

I know firsthand of a few other cures that use weeds,
like the one for John's wart and the cure for burns from
the leaves of the rabbit ear plant soaked in olive oil. Both
these remedies came from Provence, where I think that
everything that springs from its earth, here rust-red
where the vanquished Saracens dyed it with their infidel
blood, there gray with powdered marble and granite or
bright white with salt, every single tough odorous leaf
and stem is known intimately by the people of the country.

There is not a flower in the wild hills or the tamest
gardens there without some quality of cure in it, whether dried, powdered, steeped, inhaled, pounded. Usually
men and beasts eat the same plants, and for much the
same reasons, but occasionally there is one like the au-

tumn crocus, which cattle shun, but which is an active remedy in folk medicine against the gout.

Another cure I learned firsthand on the farm near Aix was for bad insect bites. It was a kind of rune in the dialect that Gaby the farmer's wife used, part Provençal and part Piedmontese, but I cannot rhyme it in my own language.

She sang it out in a rough shout when her husband came running into the courtyard from the olive orchard, rolling up his trouser-leg as he stumbled along. He yelled something at her, and "A scorpion bite . . . he's been bitten!" she cried out. She yelled, then, the rhyme at us, and when we did not understand she ran off herself and came straight back with a handful of leaves, which she scrubbed hard against the part of the farmer's foot where we could see a white blotch already formed from the bite, with pinkening skin around it. The crushed leaves made a greenish stain.

He grinned at us and his cursing died off, and we all drank a cool beer.

Once he had gone back to the orchard, Gaby taught me the remedy in her bad French, which still sang as she repeated it. Here is the only way I can write it, but it is good anyway, a perfect combination of superstition, instinct, and primitive knowledge which may well be part of our own pharmacopeia, for all I know:

Sure Cure for a Scorpion Bite

Run fast and find three kinds of leaves, one jagged (like the dandelion), one round, and one long. Crush them in your hand and rub them hard over the bitten place. Rub rub *rub*.

"Or if you can't find any leaves," Gaby said, "Rub rub *rub* with plenty of good wine vinegar. Same for wasp stings, bee stings. Or any plain brandy . . . But the three leaves work the best."

Another cure that needs leaves came to me from Tahiti, through the Italian who was raised in the Brazilian jungle and made delicious drinks for me in an air-conditioned Tahitian hut in California. It was used in Mexico too, he said, and the only difference was how to pronounce the plant: *wah*-bah south of the Border, and gou-*ah*-vah in the Islands.

"This is sure-fire for any bleeding at all," he said firmly over his refilled glass. "Deep cuts even. But you must have plenty of juice, that's it. Fill your mouth with tender guava leaves and chew them to a soft paste, and put them on the cut. Also for sores. The spit, if you will forgive my bad word, is what is the sure-fire. If you have guava leaves of course!"

And still another leaf cure, from Mexico, was told me by Nigel, who for a long time lived in Ajijic on the Lake of Chapala. It too uses a plant which animals will not touch, like the cows, even when the lake is dry and they are dying of thirst, a bush called the "gigante." Its cool green leaves when bound upon the forehead will cure any kind of headache, as well as soothe a fever.

This seems more logical to me than another receipt I copied a long time ago from one of the oldest collections of such medicaments that I have ever seen, called *A Booke of Phisical Recepts*. I would hate to have to drink this concoction, but I like the title:

Mrs. Sherlock's recept for a pain in ye head

2 ounses of Rubbarb leaves sliced, 1 ounse of Jensit's bark in powder, 2 ounses of sugar candy, 2 drams of Juniper Berris, Sinamon & nutmeg of each a dram: a Quart of strong wine infuse it in.

XIV

If you prick us, do we not bleed? if
you tickle us, do we not laugh? if you
poison us, do we not die? and if you
wrong us, shall we not revenge?
Shakespeare

There are two more things I know at first or perhaps
near-second hand, about how to stop bleeding. It is odd
to me that both of them came from Negroes.

One of them was used by a Negro to save a white
child, with human spit but no gou-*ah*-vah leaves. The
other was used by white doctors to save a Negro woman
who had learned the same remedy from her ancestors.

The first case happened the longest ago, perhaps sev-
enty-five years, but the white man who told it to me
still had bewilderment in his voice. A cousin came to
visit him, he said, on the farm in Delaware. She was like
a lovely fragile doll, with the palest skin he had ever
seen, and silvery hair that fell in a soft cape over her little
shoulders.

Everything about the farm was strange to her, and he led her by the hand from one marvel to another. Behind them always was black Tom. They watched lambs in the meadow by the great river, and Tom held the ewe while they straddled her for a short bumpy ride. They stood under the cherry trees and caught fruit in their hands when Tom shook the heavy branches.

Then once they went alone into the enormous dim barn. The man who told me this could not remember if his little cousin fell, but suddenly there she was, standing in wonder as red blood spurted out of her wrist from a long cut. The boy screamed *"Tom!"* and Tom was there from the shadows, and what happened next took perhaps seconds but not minutes, while Tom pinched the little girl's arm and the boy swept from the walls and rafters of the dim old barn great vague floating masses of cobwebs. They were gray with dust and age. They were without weight.

"More, more. Fast," the Negro commanded, as the little boy put the tenuous stuff into his free hand. He rolled it lightly into wads, and stuffed it against the deep cut on the little girl's arm. She watched without a sound. Tom packed the cobwebs as far as he could push them into her flesh. Then he took the last handful and spat into it and made a kind of plaster of it and put it over the wound. All the bleeding had stopped, but there was blood on the barn floor, plenty of it.

Tom took the little doll-like cousin into his arms and sat down with her against the hay, and sent the boy up to the Big House for a clean bandage and refreshments.

"You tell Maidie Miss Anne cut herself a little but all is well. Tell her Tom says so. You tell Maidie we could use some of her best eggnog, if she can spare the time. And you bring back a little clean bandage, boy, to cover us up."

The way it was told to me, Tom left the cobwebs in the wound, under the neat bandaging, and then removed them the next day. Nothing was ever said about how or why the cousin hurt herself, but there were two things about it that the little boy never told his mother: Tom's wife Maidie sent them an eggnog so well laced with good bourbon that all three of them drank it and slept in the hay, close together, for a good two hours; and Tom said, 'Don't you two ever tell that I spat in the cobwebs, hear me?'

They never did, but it puzzled the boy until he was very old that a Negro could save the life of a white child, and not want the whites to know that his own spittle had entered into her blood, along with the dust and spider tissue. In fact, he died still puzzled, still wondering why he had been weak enough, or even stubborn enough, to heed black Tom's request.

And in the second case of a good cure for bleeding, a fine Negro woman was in a way hoist on her own petard, for she swore that nobody but her Gramma knew the best way to cure a nosebleed, and she was proved wrong.

She lived in Pasadena, on Sugar Hill, and no life was more dramatic than hers. She was technically a "cleaning woman," with hours and even half-days promised here and there to white faculty wives, between her bouts with the medical profession. She was such a monumentally excellent servant as well as so exciting as a disaster-prone raconteuse that her employers paid her double, and put up with all her alcoholic and institutional absences, just to hear her recount them as she dusted and swept.

She was handsome to look at—a tall ferocious woman with the thin nose of a high-born Abyssinian. Her skin was coppery-black. She wore her hair in a regal pouf on top of her small head. Her gestures were as deft as those of a Chinese goldsmith while she mopped and talked of what had last happened to her at the hospital.

She was a historic figure there. It was said among the fashionable internes that they could recognize the tone of the ambulance siren when she was in it, and if she was in the throes of a miscarriage it was always with *three* little unborn creatures, not one; if she had just been stabbed, *all* her arteries were pierced; if she was dead-drunk, every facility of the great hospital would be needed, from oxygen to adrenalin, to save her, and every available doctor would stand by, fascinated, to watch her monumental renascence.

All these things made good conversation, and Pasadenans enlivened many a party with her latest medical tourneys. I think I came in last but best, though, because I actually saw her bow to Fate, and admit that she had exhausted the drama of Medical Emergencies.

She came into the kitchen where I sat with my cousin, who rose as if in the presence of a noble ghost and said, somewhat flatly, "I heard you were dead, Ruby."

The tall beautiful woman laughed impatiently.

"Almost, almost," she said. "Never was such a nose-bleed. I swear I lost five quarts. Ask anybody. Ask those baby doctors, that's all they are. It was everywhere. All over. Everybody was crying I was really dead, this time.

"Never did go so fast in that ambulance in my life. There I was, bleeding to death, and no way to stop it, no way at all. I sure messed up that hospital. And you know what they did?"

My cousin and I were drinking vermouth and gin, because I had just got off a plane and we were arranging family problems, and we kept right on, thankfully. Ruby's voice was like a song.

"Hah," she said in a damning way, very cold and with her fine head up. "They slipping there at that big fancy high-tone place. You know what they did? They did exactly, precisely, in every way, what my Gramma taught me in Florida. It didn't cost them exactly *nothing!* You know what they did, those nothing-but-baby-doctors?"

She leaned over us, and I felt quite shriveled by her noble long copper body, and her scorn.

"They put bacon grease up my nose."

My cousin and I had nothing to reply to this. We sat stupidly in the prim Pasadena kitchen where we were really not supposed to be at that hour and sipped the gin we were not supposed to be drinking at that hour. Ruby pulled off her coat angrily and tossed it on the electric dishwasher.

"Anybody can do that," she said. "My Gramma always did it. With a very *serious* nosebleed. And now I nearly die and they do it at that big stylish place just like we would do in Florida. They saved my life, those baby doctors, for I was surely dying. And what they do is stuff my nose with bacon fat, is all! And here I am."

She stopped being so angry, and we all began to laugh.

XV

There is no cure for birth and death,
save to enjoy the interval.
George Santayana

Some receipts, like the raw potatoes that Jack London chewed in the Klondike to help his scurvy, are completely simple: one thing to cure one ill. Another as direct as this is gin for women's monthly misery.

"Gin is our best friend, girl," a fellow sufferer informed me soberly in a coal town in Southern Illinois. "It's not the liquor in it, it's the juniper juice that does the trick."

When I asked if a plain tea, made from the little berries or their oil, would not save us from the dubious bootleg gin we had to buy in 1927, she said a mysterious but firm No. The gin helped, she said, and whether she meant the berries or us I did not understand.

(Here is a somewhat more complicated remedy for

this same complaint: white corn whiskey, or "mule," spiked with plenty of ginger and a modicum of hot water. It is called Ozark Stew, and has done much to keep mountain women happy, a happy mountain woman told me. She implied that Ozark females who manage to live past their years of childbearing owe it mostly to the stew, with snuff and the Bible rated as sure helps too.)

It is the cure-alls, though, that are the most interesting to reflect upon, as the simplest of the remedies that seem to have drifted into my life. They resemble in some ways my mother's "course of sprouts," although she never claimed that her panacea covered more than the myriad effects, many of them emotional, of a sluggish liver. Probably the simplest of them all, and the most all-embracing, is what in France is called "a little slice of ham."

Over some thirty years of fascinated observation, I have been assured that a little slice of ham, especially when taken in bed with a glass of good wine, will cure completely or at least help cure the following: exhaustion, migraine, grippe, gout, disappointment in love, business worries, childbed fever, dizziness, coughing, and indeed almost everything else except Death and Taxes.

The ham should be what we call "boiled," and what in France is named "diet-Paris-extra-fine" and whatever else sounds dainty to the person who wants it. In extreme cases it is served without the curls of sweet butter and delicately fluted little pickles that otherwise decorate and mask its stark, flabby pinkness. Usually it is a full meal in itself, complete with a discreet slice or two or three or four of fresh bread, or several crisp pieces of what we call zwieback at home. The wine that helps wash down this tidbit should not be ordinary, of course.

Perhaps the oddest thing about this prescription, besides the fact that people who follow it are as convinced as are the doctors who prescribe it that they are fasting, is that most of the hardy Frenchmen who believe so will recover.

They will not suffer from indigestion. Their livers will not shrivel in one last paroxysm of revulsion before the dainty fat slice of embalmed pork-flesh, and the salted pickles, and the mildly alcoholic flushing of the fermented grape juice. They will not, in other words, die.

(Then.)

Once more they will react to the balm of a quiet room, and of a simple meal, spiced with the extra sauce of loving care and consternation.

I have often thought with some regret of things I would like to inherit if I had been born French, but this panacea is not among them. It is too rugged for me. The few times I would have been deemed ready for it I was past wanting or needing anything but the prerequisite, the quiet room.

But I suspect that the sturdiness of the nation may stem from it, even if considered as somewhat the same test as the Spartan one, where a sick or spindly soldier was subjected to a drink made of warm ale, herbs, and iron filings: if he spewed it out or rolled up and died, he was still a boy, no man. If Frenchmen can survive the routine prescription given from Dover to Marseille, and can eat all the little slices of ham prescribed for them as they lie languishing, they will outlast many another Austerlitz.

Me, I think I prefer some such receipt as this following one, at least in contemplation. It promises to cure many things, and implies the easing of as many more.

It was first noted in a book by a pre-Elizabethan midwife named Dame Lethiculear, who most certainly soothed many more ills than the fleeting ones of childbirth. Its spelling is not ours, and it seems to go into a song which has in it all the magic, the atavistic knowledge, and the mixture of faith and good sense which are compounded in real medicine.

To make ye Green Ointment that cured Lady Probyn's Coachman's Back

Take of Sage and Rue of each one handfull, and of
    wormwood and leaves of bay
Each half a pound.
Gather these in the heat of Day, and leave them
All unwashed and Shreded small. Then take of
Sheep suet one pound and a half, and stamp it with
    the herbs
Until they be all of one couler.
Put into it one pint and a half
Of the best Sallet Oil from Spain.
Then stir all well together,
And put it in a pot,
And stop it close up,
And let it stop nine days.

Boil it then,
Till the strength of the herb be gone,
And take care in thus boiling that you doe not burn it.
Then of the oil of Spike add one ounse and a half
And keep it for your use.
It is good for all manner of wounds,
Of Bruises, of burns and sprains,
And the best time to make it is in the month of May.

XVI

"But wait a bit," the Oysters cried,
  "Before we have our chat;
For some of us are out of breath,
  And all of us are fat!"
                              Lewis Carroll

The fine line between use and abuse cannot perhaps be clearer than in the human history of weight control. Depending upon the fashions in clothes, our preoccupation with it can change with hysterical speed to pure obsession, and it has been too easy, from the earliest times in history, for sad or scoffing writers to list the atrocities committed in the name of slenderness. Most of them, in one form or another, involve plain starvation.

It is rare to see a fat poor man, unless his obesity comes from an imbalance in his glands or from unhappiness. Most poor people, like most poor nations, are thin.

The United States, now, is very rich, and while statistics are basically to be distrusted, they are at least a superficial indication, currently, that there are more deaths from heart attacks in America, and more collapses from fad diets, than in any other country in the world. In other words, we eat too much, and then like all young ignorant peoples, we exaggerate our efforts to grow slim and well again.

Of course not all fat people have heart attacks, but nobody can deny that a heart which has to keep two hundred and fifty pounds of body alive must work harder than one with half that much to maintain.

On the other hand, many human hearts stop under the strain of foolhardy dieting to keep a body thin, and all of us know of actresses, or second cousins, who have fallen dead on their bathroom scales, slim and beautiful and exhausted.

Perhaps death is preferable to living in the constant shadow of obesity, if one must be professionally svelte.

I know a woman who is even-natured and gay when she weighs exactly twenty pounds more than her studio contract will permit, and who becomes suicidal when she lives on the pills and stimulants that keep her a financial as well as photogenic asset. She is a real artist, so she stays thin and lives in Hell. Doctors help her past the outer edges of their Hippocratic oath, with pity. Her talent is worth saving, to inspire less gifted mortals.

They, usually less aided by the knowing, often destroy themselves in much the same way, trying for their own reasons to stay lovely.

When I was young, I never thought this way or that about my own ounces and pounds, but I pondered the reason why my most beautiful cousin, the one who was still the Family Belle, slept in a bed raised several inches at the foot. It was, we all knew, because she had sent secretly for a nostrum while she was in boarding school, fearing that she would be too plump for the Christmas balls.

She took the pills, which may have contained worm seeds in them to deceive her. She did indeed lose several pounds. But before the holidays were over she collapsed, her insides as flaccid as a punctured balloon, no longer able to hold themselves where they must stay for childbearing, or for even the routine duties of a human body.

It was a pity. She should have known better. Her father was a doctor.

Most doctors, for hundreds of years, have urged people not to get fat, but if they have let this happen, to reduce their weight gradually and sanely. Some have turned, and still do, to the animals: Eat when you are hungry, eat according to the seasons of the year, and always rest afterwards. This is what cats do, and dogs and mice.

Cats are perhaps the most like us, in that they will gormandize until they must vomit painfully what they have swallowed for pure pleasure. But they never grow fat unless they are too protected and made lazy and careless by us, the human beings.

Animals that sleep in the winter emerge with most of their fat gone, and then refresh themselves with tonic weeds and berries before the strenuous mating season. Men are less obvious than this, but still feel an atavistic hunger for green leaves in the spring, or bracing purges:

spinach and dandelions and mustard, sulfur-and-molasses, or something like this liver-restorative which was told me by a nun in Switzerland:

> One teaspoon of sulfate of soda in a glass of water, every three days for the month of February or March, to be taken a half-hour before breakfast.

(She also told me that the best thing in the world for a dull liver, in the spring or any time, is to rest for a few minutes after every meal with a hot water bottle on one's stomach. This sounds very pleasant.)

A good way to cut down hunger, I have been told, is to chew on a couple of elm leaves, or on almost any leaves which are rough and with jagged edges. For some reason they all seem to have a taste or texture which will occupy a hungry farmer, for instance, enough to make him forget that it is three hours to dinner.

Another good way to stave off the rigors of feeling famished is to drink something very thin and watery, like cold weak coffee from a bottle, or wine cut with at least five times its amount of water, or water with a little vinegar in it.

This is true at the table as well, and people who wish to lose a little weight slowly but surely have proved that it can be done if at each meal they will sip a glass of water with one or two teaspoons of apple cider vinegar or wine vinegar in it. ("Lose a half-pound a month, and *keep* it lost," a wise good doctor once said slyly to me.)

All these flat sourish suggestions sound boring or actively unpleasant, but being too fat is even more so.

Perhaps the most poignant story of a foolish girl's mis-use of vinegar to cut her appetite, and one that always reminds me of my beautiful cousin because of the horrid secrecy of it, is in Brillat-Savarin's *Physiology of Taste.* It is doubly real, perhaps, because it is his one admission of personal ardor in a book famous for its reticence.

Louise, he wrote, was one of the loveliest people he could ever remember knowing, who "possessed in per-fect proportions that classical plumpness which has al-ways charmed man's eyes and added richness to his arts." But some of her friends teased her about the risk of grow-ing fat, and secretly for one month she drank a glass of vinegar every morning. By the time she confessed to it, "there was no hope left . . . victim of stupid advice, the lovely Louise, reduced to the shocking state caused al-ways by consumption, went to sleep for all eternity when she was but barely eighteen years old."

Perhaps it was this early sadness that made the old lawyer ponder deeply on the dangers of obesity, and write wittily about them. Some of his preventives are more than merely odd to us, but always interesting to consider. He prescribed thirty bottles of Seltzer water, for instance, to be drunk before meals during the sum-mer. This seems sensible enough . . . but he also advised drinking a large cup of strong hot chocolate after a hearty breakfast to maintain one's correct weight and to digest properly in time for an equally hearty dinner!

An anti-fat belt was another of his pet prescriptions, to support the belly and to act "as a warning sentinel when one had eaten too much."

I have often seen a version of this cinched onto exquisite starlets and "stock girls" in Hollywood, when they must supply their press agents' version of America's Paper-Towel Industry Queens at 100-Dollars-a-Plate banquets for visiting executives without risking the studio's investment in their silhouettes.

Unlike the old Frenchman's pattern, to hold a fattened body gently constricted, day and night, until sensible diet has made the belt unnecessary, the hasty torture of the Hollywood version, as crude as a medieval chastity belt, has worn lines of tired pain on many pretty faces in "the industry," and sent otherwise fairly normal appetites into an hysterical foolish guzzling, once the banquets are over and the cinches off. Young healthy females, no matter how ethereal they appear in public, will eat like horses in private, especially if they are worked like horses too . . .

Quinine was another substance which Brillat-Savarin believed to be actively anti-fat, and he recommended it as an infallible preventive if used sensibly.

He suggested one month of judicious dieting, and then one month of this rigid pattern: every other day at exactly seven in the morning, a glass of dry white wine in which has been dissolved about a teaspoonful of good red quinine. "Excellent results will follow," he said.

It is impossible for me to imagine this potion, for I know little about quinine except that it is said to be very bitter. It is also used in appetite-provokers like vermouth, which would seem to me to defeat its purpose of helping people lose weight, unless the professor's suspicion be correct, that its tannic content closes off the cells that might horde fat. Perhaps the wisest of his conclusions about obesity is that "the severer a diet may be, the less effect it will have." He was not a real doctor, but he might well have been, and today as then, and as much farther back in Time, wisdom like his has advised moderation in most of the preventives as well as the cures that we must follow to remain upright and comparatively at ease.

XVII

Love is a sickness, full of woes,
All remedies refusing.
Samuel Daniel

It is easy to understand most of the magic, and even some of the medicine, in receipts which come from the far days when men were closer to their animal companions and could draw more counsel from them than we do, now that mechanization has taken command.

Some people still follow, no matter how unthinkingly, lessons they first learned hundreds of years ago, and just as bears coming out of their winter sleep will eat mightily of certain leaves and berries to awaken themselves for the time of frolicking and love, so country people instinctively eat such things as dandelions in the spring, in soups and salads, boiled or wilted as a vegetable, kegged the year before as a wine, brewed as a tonic . . .

Dandelions are rich in salts and oils, and a broth made from them has long been drunk to prevent various skin diseases, mostly the kinds resulting from poor winter diets. They act as a diuretic, and are believed to cleanse the liver by stimulating the flow of bile . . . all this in the turbid springtime, when everything prepares itself for rebirth.

And even in 1961, scientists as far apart as Greece and England continue to ponder on the peculiar sex life of this pretty little herb, which like the snail and the oyster seems able to be both male and female, and to give birth to fertile yellow flowers which turn into the spun-glass mysterious floating things all children know. The process is called parthenogenesis, I think—a noble word, no matter what strange activities it may imply.

It may explain very indirectly the special magic of the dandelion, in some parts of Europe, to tell when a maiden will be married. I know girls in Provence who are only half laughing when they blow on a dandelion flower when it is full of seeds . . . and watch the lovely things float off. If only one seed holds tightly to the base of the flower, then within only one short year . . . but the maiden must blow hard and wish fiercely.

XVIII

If thou be hurt with horn of hart,
  It brings thee to thy bier.
But barber's hand shall boar's hurt
  heal.
  Therefore, have lesser fear.
  Fifteenth-century Doggerel

In the thirteenth century in Europe, when we lived close to the wild creatures and hunted them for their meat and their skins, men often modeled themselves upon their best enemies, and with true respect believed that they could gain courage if they ate a brave bear's heart, fleetness if they ate the powdered hooves of a gazelle.

The deer was held to be the healthiest of all forest animals, and people felt that they should eat as much of its flesh as possible to remain well. (It is plain that huntsmen lived far from the stinking towns where the plague was an endemic prowler, and that they subsisted on venison. *Ergo,* the wild meat protected them from the plague!)

In case fevers might attack even the sturdy hunters, they could be prevented by drinking with hot wine or ale the powdered marrow of a stag's right horn, which is more powerful and therefore more efficacious than its left. This preventive was an obvious one in 1250 A.D., when it was noted in a bestiary: every hunter believed in those days that a stag never has a fever, and that his strongest part will perforce contain the most of what protects him.

With the same reasoning many people in this very winter of today wear, either boldly or with some slight embarrassment at being so "old-fashioned," a cat's furry pelt on their chests. They may think it is because their grandmothers taught them to, or because cat skins are a cheap protection against the winter winds, but the real reason is that in 1200 or 1600 people still believed that cats, leopards, lions, and all other felines were immune to colds and inflammations of the chest.

Even in astrology, men born under the sign of Leo held firmly and conveniently to either of these rules: (1) they were utterly safe from all such ailments, or (2) they were especially sensitive to them and must therefore protect themselves with the symbolic covering.

Now, in Western Europe at least, with the first proofs of real winter the pharmacy windows show forth their finest pelts, to shock even the least squeamish of the cat-lovers and send children guessing as to how and where they were come by. Are there old men who trap unwary housecats on the rooftops and skin them to sell? Is it a respectable trade, or something hidden, and if hidden, in what stinking loft or cellar are the skins dried to such a softness? Where did the cats come from?

That last is the most agonizing part of the puzzlement, and is best passed over quickly by the sensitive, the true ailurophiles. The fact remains that cat skins are worn by countless people, to protect their chests from winter winds and, more atavistically, to lend some of their magic animal immunity to the spindly humans who depend upon it.

There may be something of this same curative magic, this optimistic identification, in the custom in high Swiss villages of saving the fat of the female marmots to give to women after childbirth.

Marmots are odd and gentle little rodents, protected now by the Swiss government because they sit trustingly while hunters knock them dead for sport. There are a few left in the mountains, and I have been told that they are heart-warming to watch, very tender, with tidy family habits in spite of their extravagant fertility, and with inevitably healthy, gay children, one litter after another.

The folk logic in the use of their fat for women after birthing is obvious, at least to Swiss villagers. Mother marmots, who seem to take great pleasure in romping from one delivery to the next, always gay and healthy, are especially fat between times. Is it not the fat that makes them so? Then give it to women, so that they too will recover gaily and healthily from childbed and be ready again!

The fat is sweet as a nut and will stay so from one year to the next, in a clean jar—and since it is necessary now and then to kill the little marmot-mothers to obtain it, thrifty Swiss mountaineers make a good feast as well, a special stew to be served with the best wine in the house, for weddings and engagements and, most appropriate of all, for christenings.

I myself have never seen one of these little animals, much less tasted its sweet fat or its tender flesh, but I was told of their happy medicine by a man in Zermatt who was respected for the fifty years he had been a mountain guide.

He was sitting in the sun, as all men that old should do, although not many sit on a snowbank as easily as he. He began to dig into it, and pound at it where it was packed, and gradually with me helping him we dug down to the heads of two bronze marmots, who smiled up mischievously, very black in the snow. They were part of the town fountain, which was always covered when I passed it.

Later the old guide showed me a summer picture of it, in his little ski-shop. It was frolicsome and pretty, with a family of the plump creatures playing on some rocks, large as life, modeled by a famous native sculptor.

The old man said he had often hunted marmots when he was a boy. He told me of their magical fat. It would make any new mother strong and happy, he said, and eager to have another child. *Naturally!*

XIX

I am sick as a horse.

Laurence Sterne

As always, one thing leads to another, and one or two receipts connected with pregnancy seem indicated here.

One was told me, indeed recommended, by a doctor so truly great that he has been able to achieve simplicity. He was talking about the unnecessary qualms of morning sickness, real no matter how psychogenic, especially in young mothers.

"The female body is fighting to protect its fetus," he said impatiently. "It needs a chance. It has to expel excess acids that have collected during the night. A woman who is run down or malnourished will make more noxious acids than a healthy one who is not toxic, but even a well-fed girl may feel queasy for a time when she starts a baby. She should drink some water with a little baking soda in it, a teaspoonful to a glass, and slowly. If she ought to vomit, the soda water will make it easier. If she does not really need to expel the acids, the soda will neutralize them and stop her queasiness. It is simple; either way, she'll feel better . . ."

Somewhat this same process has been described in a book about Vermont folk medicine, in which pregnant women are advised to sip a glassful of water containing one teaspoonful of apple-cider vinegar while they dress in the morning. A pure wine vinegar will do almost as well as the one made from apples, and of course the slow gentle swallowing has its own medicine, and helps keep one's mind off the unpleasant aspects of a heaving stomach, in pregnancy as well as in any other kind of nausea.

XX

Give me an ounce of civet, good
apothecary, to sweeten my
imagination.

Shakespeare

As a restorative rather than a preventive, the slow sipping of water either plain or with a little honey or sugar
in it has helped many a case of severe vomiting after one
has eaten something poisonous: it stays down, to put it
bluntly, and the rhythm of taking a teaspoonful every
three minutes, or five, acts as a kind of medicinal lullaby.

This is true in cases of depression and panic, too. Once
in my own life when I was waiting for something but
was not sure what or why, and therefore showed a few of
the signs of apprehension which doctors perhaps mistak-
enly associate with "the stress of modern life," I got myself through many a near crisis by taking three sips, ex-

actly three, from a glassful of water with exactly one tea-spoon of soda in it, exactly every fifteen minutes.

There is good medical sense in this, if one holds with the theory that psychological conditions are induced or at least abetted by toxic states. The soda neutralizes many of the excitants and intoxicants in the stomach, and so on. And of course the moral obligation to do a certain thing at a certain time helps to hold a frightened person to a reassuring rhythm until his poor tense nervous system has had time to calm itself. Or so I found, and so I have told other people in a puzzlement.

An older phrase for such a state is the "lowness of Spirrits" that apothecaries of Shakespeare's times treated with something like this receipt:

Dr. Lowrer's Drops

Take a pint of the best Brandy and put into it one ounce of Assafetida Bruised, with 2 Spoonfulls of Wood soot. Set this in a Bottle for 9 or 10 days and nights near a fire . . . For Lowness of Spirrits take 15, 20, or 30 Drops in White wine or Black Cherry water, twice a day, and increase the Dose till you come to a Teaspoonfull. 'Tis most admirable to strengthen the Nerves also, or for Gidiness in the Head.

The foul-smelling stuff which I first called assafeddity, taught by my little friend Bertha who wore it about her neck to ward off human ills, was much used by doctors in the old days to cheer and comfort people, and I have several other receipts for the Renaissance neurotics which call for it. Here is one for

High Spirrited Pills

Salt of Steel	
Galbmam (?) strain'd	of each 3 drams
Castor (the finest sort)	
Assafeetida	
Salt of Amber	of each 2 Scruples
Camphire	

Make all these into little Pills & take 3 at Night & 3 at Morn, with a little bitters after them.

I wonder if this Salt of Amber is like the tincture of amber mentioned in old recipes for aphrodisiacs, or the "piece of amber the size of a bean" which Brillat-Savarin used to pound with some sugar and stir into a cup of hot strong chocolate to cure his occasional gloom and clear his head?

This must have been toward the end of his life, for he confessed that he most often drank his restorative when he had hit on one of those days when the weight of age lay heavily upon him, and said, "Thanks to [it] the mechanics of living grow easier, my mind works quickly, and I do not suffer from the insomnia which would be the inevitable result of taking a cup of black coffee for the same purpose." He died in 1826, a year after his *Physiology of Taste* was published, an old man.

Any man who can depend upon a tonic for help in his last years, for those days when the "weight of age" seems heavier than usual, has the right to a few peculiarities, whether they include powdered amber or not.

Many of us imitate our friends the animals; we move more slowly, and sleep more peacefully in the warm corner by the hearth. Few of us, though, go as far as to emulate the aging stag, at least as he is told about in a thirteenth century bestiary:

"When the stag feels that he grows old and stiff, he seeks the lair of his enemy, a snake. With his great nostrils he sucks forth the serpent, and devours him whole. The eating of the venemous snake restores the mighty animal's health, and he then sheds his old skin and is young again."

I have seen toad and cobra venom injected to prevent pain, with only questionable results, and I have read of the curative powers of "snake-oil" in old advertisements for rheumatism quackeries, but I have yet to find any preventive but this beastly one for the rejuvenation of an aging stag. Men are perhaps less cognizant of their actual state than the mighty males of the forest?

Perhaps they need more help, more gentleness. Perhaps they must wait for the care of such a daughter-in-law as had the King of Colchicum, who brewed for her sovereign a philter of thousands of crocus flowers. It was said afterwards that the old king, weary, worn, and ready to die, grew younger by at least forty years.

Crocuses have figured in man's medicine for hundreds of years, although they are one of the herbs that beasts shun, whether in the naked pale lavender flower or in the spindly leaves that follow. In France and Switzerland peasants called them "dog-killers." They grow in sickly meadowland, and in the moist dead pockets formed in little mountain valleys by glaciers that have long since vanished. *"Colchicum autumnale,"* the pharmacists call

them, and today as long ago they are one of the best specifics against gout.

Modern doctors repeat what the old folk medicine has
always said, that they must be used with care, for they
are powerfully stimulating to bad as well as good hu-
mors in the human body . . . dog-killer can be man-
killer!

Derivatives of the autumn crocus are much used in the
modern pharmacopeia, not only as antispasmodics, but
to inhibit virus multiplication. In spite of our current
preoccupation with the problems of aging, though, I
have not yet heard that anything has been done to put
back the clock for senior citizens as did the solicitous
daughter-in-law of the old tired King of Colchicum.
Perhaps her recipe is still too simple for us.

XXI

Give strong drink to them that are sad
. . . Let them drink, and forget their
want.

Proverbs 31:6, 7

Cordials and elixirs, though, have long been used to make men feel younger, as well as stronger, wiser, calmer, gentler, and many other things. All of them are to be drunk, which in itself is a soothing act; an angry or excited throat is too constricted to swallow with any comfort. Most of them are made of a varying intricacy of herbs and essences, and most of them contain some kind of alcohol.

Here is the most innocent of any I know about, an honest compromise between fear of the Demon Alcohol and a natural need for occasional stimulation. It has been recommended to me by a woman who bows to the former and the latter with almost equal grace and discretion.

When she is tired and bored and old-ish, and even the good sun beats meanly on her shoulders, she brews herself, for one day, this potion on the day before:

California Tea

> Two teaspoonfuls good black tea leaves
> One quart cool water
> One sprig mint

Blend, put in glass jar, and let stand in the hot sun four or five hours. Strain, cool, and drink within a day or so, with some honey if desired.

A drink that is less stimulating than this oddly potent brew, but with its innocence, is one familiar to most farmers of New England, especially in haying times. It used to be mixed in big crocks, I have been told, and carried out to the fields in midmorning and midafternoon by the strongest prettiest farm girls: fresh, cool well water, and a good cup of apple cider vinegar and some honey for every gallon of it.

This made a sharp-sweet potion much like the "tonic" which is currently stylish in America: one teaspoon of good honey, one of Vermont vinegar, in a glass of water two or three times a day at meals, to work miracles ranging soberly from an increased birth rate to freedom from postnasal drip.

Such potables give the lie to the theory, perhaps a thousand years old, that volatile alcohol adds much to the efficacy of all tonics, elixirs, extracts, bitters, and cordials meant to succor men. Nevertheless, the "aqua vitae" that the alchemists discovered in the Dark Ages, no matter how disguised, is an essential part of most such drinks, and to my mind at least it adds enjoyably to their employment.

During and then after the time when monasteries were the refuge of scholars and poets as well as men of God, it was inevitable that the Flesh and Devil raised as many problems there as did the Spirit, and many receipts for quieting them are still used today, in the elixirs that the holy fathers evolved in their kitchens. We call some of them liqueurs, and serve them after our more fastuous meals: Benedictine, Chartreuse.

And there are countless others known only locally, such as the oily potent brew made in Provence and called Senancole for the Abbey of Senanque, or Arquebuse, made by the Marist Brothers in a Rhône village, and proudly recommended by them for both internal and external use.

Arquebuse, according to its label, can be rubbed upon the skin to prevent swelling after sprains or insect bites, or blue bruise marks after a fall or a fight, and it will also prevent infection if diluted and swabbed upon even the dirtiest wounds.

Taken internally, it will work wonders too. In a grog it quickly dissipates a chill and thus avoids grippes and even pneumonia; a teaspoonful night and morning in a little sugared water will aid the circulation, and before bedtime guarantees sweet sleep; taken pure, or in a tea, or even on a lump of sugar, it will prevent stomachache, cramps, nausea, and all kinds of indigestion, such as that due to overeating.

The little label says flatly of Arquebuse that it is *indispensable.* Myself, I have found it an excellent preventive for two things: rubbed upon the skin it seems to ward off insects, and taken in one or two nips it quiets the mixture of queasiness and apprehension that seem to plague many travelers before embarking, especially for a plane trip.

The last time I was told this, I had given a pocket flask of Arquebuse to a friend about to take off over the North Pole from Europe to San Francisco, and she wrote to me from her home port, on a postcard of the Golden Gate, "Thank you for elixir of Marist Brothers . . . took a couple of swigs on departure and landing. *Vita nuova.*"

All such claims can be made for most herbal and vegetal elixirs, but the lesser-known brands of them seem to be stronger, less cloying, more plainly aromatic. This is even truer of the "home-made" kinds, which still bolster country people everywhere, without benefit of modern or even of monkish apothecaries.

I know two excellent recipes, one from the mountains of Switzerland where I once lived and the other from a friend in the mountains of Colorado, where she has lived for almost a hundred years. They both make excellent digestive bitters, to be used as well for medicine as for pleasure.

The first I learned from the villagers who helped me cull the summer fruits into big barrels in the orchard, and then bottle the rank alcohol that was distilled from their rotting juices.

Some of us stuffed herbs into the bottles of this distillation, and made a kind of *digestif* from it, the simplest way. Others went to more lengths, and their cordials and "essences" were very good indeed.

Here is one using flowers and roots from the mountain meadows, which I have never made myself, although I have helped with the plant-gathering and the bottling, and have tasted somewhat more than my fair share, since I so obviously did not *need* it.

It is used both to aid digestion in convalescence and to excite it in any state at all, and even when unnecessary it is a pleasant variation on the act of swallowing:

Take the flowers of at least 15 kinds of meadow plants, and the roots of at least five more, such as Peony, Licorice, and Hepatica. Clean and slice them finely, and cover them with white wine, to steep three days. Stir well, night and morning. Bring to the boil, and strain.

Mix with equal parts of fine honey and with five parts of good fruit brandy. Store in a wooden cask for one year, and bottle. Drink cold or lukewarm on an empty stomach, to restore appetite, or on a full one, to encourage it.

The receipt from the Far West starts out, "Take 12 quart bottles of the best bourbon whiskey," but I can easily decode it into a puny pint-sized formula for moderners with less Gargantuan propensities and shelf space:

Mrs. Lackner's Mountain Bitters

Take Western sage blossoms, which must be gathered thoroughly dried and cured in the sun, and pack them into an empty pint bottle to the depth of two inches or more. Add to this the peel of one lemon which has been detached from its fruit and thoroughly dried in the sun. Fill the bottle to the top with good bourbon, and let stand for at least two weeks before using . . . the longer the better.

This simple elixir, which like Arquebuse has no sugar added to it, is "just dandy for almost anything," Mrs. Lackner says, but especially as a year-in-year-out tonic, to be taken night and morning, a small nip. To continue in her lingo, "It's good for what ails you," with a modicum of common sense added, of course! It would not heal a broken bone nor prevent a cancer . . .

There are other more concentrated bitters, innocent of sweetening if not of aqua vitae. For various reasons, some more obvious than others, mountaineers like the Swiss concoct them: they must stand up to the affront of icy cold; they must use the beneficent summer meadow herbs during their violently short season of ripe flowering, and so on. I remember one called something like Dennler-Alpen bitters, which taken in a half-filled cup of hot water would raise the hair on a bald hound-dog. It would and does send shuddering mountain people and even skiers happily out into the snow.

This is somewhat like the Italian Fernet-Branca, which smells and looks like the epitome of the old Arabian recipe for coffee: black as night, hot as Hell, etc., etc.

The first time I ever saw these bitters actually used, and not placed expectantly on a bar, was at about 11:30 of the morning in a worldly pub, when one of the most electrically attractive men I have ever imagined came in, straight and blind as a poised and desperate bee, and drank down in one expert gulp a shot glass of it.

It was not until he had swallowed it that I understood that he had been dying on his feet, for in a magical way I saw him turn from a zombi to a live man as the vile stuff took hold in him. Within a few seconds he became real, and of course somewhat less mysteriously alluring, but more acceptable.

The last time I considered the strange possibilities of this bitters, whose addicts imply that it is everything from a carminative to a preventive of gout, was not long ago. A barman whom I have long known and much admired, now plainly on his last legs, talked ruminatively of things he had learned in his philosophical employment. I got around gradually to telling him of the morning when I had watched the potential Dream walk, stiff as a plank, past if not into my life.

He smiled as only a Spaniard can, and said, "He was probably a headwaiter or top bar man. It is a professional trick with us. We must be on our feet, and we never have time to eat like the rest of you. We live on a snatch here, a nibble there. So we eat a sandwich or omelet quickly behind the screen, and then we down a slug of Fernet. It will digest anything, anything at all, in ten minutes. We live on it."

I thought of the opposite of this lightning action as a digestive. I had read it a long time ago in a book about English mountebanks.

One of these clowns, most probably a pre-Elizabethan, was called Mr. Marryott, and he went about the countryside eating more than anyone else, and being paid for it, somewhat as modern prep-school boys have contests to swallow the most water, or pie, or goldfish, for a prize to help swell the soccer-ball fund. This is what the fellow did, in order to digest one mad meal and prepare himself for the next.

Why He Swallows Bullets and Stones

The heat of his Stomack is such, that without this Remedy he could not subsist, for when he hath gormondized himself at some great Feast, strait way he swallows bullets of almost 4 Ounses weight, which causes a present digestion: also round pebble stones he often swallows, which cools his Maw. These kind of tricks he hath, by which he puts down many of our new Juglers now a days, who will be an hour eating of a Cheese-cake; he vanquisheth all that dare oppose him in his Art.

The same barman who told me of his hidden dependence upon bitters told me also that the reason most men of Provence and all the south of France are hard as iron, sturdy as oak, and urgent as the Mistral itself, is that they drink *pastis*.

Committees for the de-alcoholization of the French working classes would shudder at this firm statement if they were in a position to hear it made; *pastis* is the grandchild, legitimate no matter how emasculated, of the absinthe that once ate caves and whirlpools in the brains of such great poets as Verlaine. It is still a cloudy fluid when the all-essential water is added to it. It still tastes and smells like the anise that once masked the wormwood in it. It is still pleasant to drink.

And according to my weary friend, men of Provence, especially outside of the towns, drink up to fifteen or even thirty small nips of it a day, cut with well water. It is a *digestif,* he assured me solemnly, and a tonic, and a preventive. It is also a preservative and a fortifier. I refrained from looking at his own worn shaking carcass, and confessed to him that although I am a woman, I too like a *pastis* now and then. This warmed his heart, if possible, and he smiled a ghastly smile at me.

"Many Provençales," he said, "enjoy a little glass of *pastis* now and then. But in general they draw female strength from the tomato, raw or cooked. It protects them from the salts in the air. It makes them more womanly. Men need to be stronger, more like lions. They need plenty of *pastis.*"

I thought of a report I once read, of a man who decided to imitate the lion in his own otherwise tidy pattern of living as a scholar in London. This was perhaps two hundred years ago.

His name was Dr. George Fordyce, from the gossip about him that can still be gleaned from contemporary diaries. He decided, toward the end of his expected span of life, that the lion was rightly king of the beasts for one high reason, his habit of eating and, more important, *drinking* but once each day.

The scholar decided to do likewise. His eccentricity was immediately of interest, needless to say, and small crowds followed his late-afternoon walk to Dolly's Chop House. As he opened the door the cook would put a big steak over the coals, and the waiter would set before the old gentleman a Gargantuan tidbit of chicken or fish and "a silver tankard of strong ale, a bottle of port, and a quarter of a pint of brandy."

All this, it is recorded, vanished in the twinkling of an eye, and I suspect that bread and cheese went along with it, as bread and potatoes do today, almost unnoticed gastronomically but nonetheless requisite as a kind of blotter.

Then the scholar downed three glasses of brandy and water at three different coffeehouses in the town, returned to his lecture room, and did not eat or drink again until his next march to Dolly's, at four the following afternoon. His lectures were notable, although by now they may be somewhat less remembered (and memorable) than his preparations for delivering them!

XXII

Better to hunt in fields, for health
unbought,
Than fee the doctor for a nauseous
draught.

John Dryden

Dr. Fordyce is believed to have lived to a very ripe and even virile age in his leonine as well as dogged pattern. Perhaps he solaced his hollow innards, if they cried for nourishment too early in the day, with a snack made somewhat after the following receipt, which was prescribed during his time for such indispositions:

How to make a Cordiall Broath

Take 3 Sheeps Hinges with the wool on their heads: 3 dozen of Sheep Trotters: 2 Bullocks Livers, with half a peck of Oat meal. Boyl all these in a Caldron 2 hours, then strain the Broath through a hair sackcloath, and let it cool. The use of it is to appease grumbling in the Guts, or a wambling stomack, by drinking one Pot at a time and eating the meat after it. This will preserve you from hunger and wind in the Stomack, using it but once in 2 hours.

This is really no odder a preventive than the one another doctor, Oliver Wendell Holmes, is said to have used faithfully to protect himself from rheumatism—a horse chestnut in one pocket of his greatcoat and a potato in the other. This receipt has a gastronomical appeal to it, too—and thriftiness as well.

Many such simple patterns, begun perhaps after an illness to restore balance to one's system, and even on the recommendation of a convincing friend, can become harmless habits, or basically endearing eccentricities, as in Dr. Holmes's case.

In my own family, for example, the whole domestic climate depended more than somewhat on whether my parents were served their "grapefruit drink" well before breakfast.

Perhaps it was self-protection that made the cook, no matter how hung-over, manage to get this potion to them. She knew as well as the rest of us that the day would be sweeter for it!

Aside from its generally salubrious effect upon the parental disposition, their grapefruit drink was rather vaguely credited with refreshing the liver, revivifying the digestion, and preventing colds. This, as I remember, was because of its mildly bitter taste, which either came from natural quinine or was believed to because quinine is bitter (a good example of the logic in most folk medicine!).

The ritual of its preparation is as clear to me as it was thirty years ago:

At night chop one ripe grapefruit (for each person) into chunks, skin and all, and cover with two cups boiling water. In the morning, strain off liquid into glass, and serve cool, to be drunk while dressing.

This makes a refreshing innocuous tipple, a good way to start the day's business in private, and my father and mother, people of very good sense and balance, felt quite thrown out of joint if not actively peevish when now and then, through carelessness, the grapefruit drink was not ready for them when they first got up in the morning.

Certainly it was a simple thing they wanted, and we always felt ashamed when because of celebrations, christenings, or wakes it was neglected.

I have often tried to cheat, but never with any luck, when in the morning I have realized that the nighttime routine had been neglected. My most successful method, which never fooled my father and which I therefore always announced as a "cheater" before he had time to point it out himself, was to chop the fruit, pour half the amount of boiling water on it, mash it, and then pour the liquid over ice cubes. It was more turgid, somewhat more bitter, and according to my politely reproachful father it did not have the same effect.

What that effect was, he never did explain, except that he "felt better" when he drank a pallid, bitter glass of the stuff. Perhaps, but at twenty-four hour intervals, it worked some of the soothing magic that the five-minute sippings of liquid will work on a poisoned stomach, or the fifteen-minute ones on a poisoned spirit?

XXIII

Keep your feet warm, your head cool,
and your bowels open.
Naval Remedy when
Ten Days from shore

Certainly a little inward bath, whether or not embit-
tered by the skin of a chopped grapefruit, can hurt nobody who will take it with some common sense, and one
convenience of the human body is that it has several
bathable apertures and entrances.

Some of them, like the ears or eyes, retain little that is
fed into them, and will reject automatically any foreign
excess. The mouth is the most retentive path for feedings
and bathings, no matter what their purpose, but at the
other end there is another good if less popular way of ac-
cess, and I know of a couple of interesting combinations
of irrigation and nourishment through its tortuous and
highly receptive walls.

One is much used by a modern doctor who is famous

for his dramatically simple success with very ill people. He often "feeds" them to hasten their recovery, by using a slow enema of from twenty to fifty per cent milk in warm water, to be retained for an hour or so. This is a cleansing and healing restorative, and the good milk neutralizes much that is toxic as it is absorbed by the delicate tissues of the bowels.

(I wonder if this milk enema might not act as a restorative after the use of some of the antibiotics, which unfortunately kill off many of the good bacilli in our intestines while they are destroying the bad ones? Most doctors who prescribe such remedies advise their patients to eat and drink yoghurt and buttermilk and yeast to help maintain some kind of balance of natural fermentation, but even so their patients are often left with lame and ravaged guts, which might possibly be soothed directly through their sensitive linings by gentle enemas—preferably of raw milk, I would guess . . .)

The other use of the enema was told me by my mother, not without some hesitation because of what seemed to her its basic indelicacy.

Perhaps if it had been about anyone not closely connected with her, or better yet, hearsay, she would not have felt so reticent. But it was about her own grandmother, a vital old character who was recalled by everyone who remembered her as part witch, part empress—a doughty Irish Victorian, who like many women of her period possessed a remarkable energy for both childbearing and religion.

When the first had run its course, she was left with all

her fervor intact and unencumbered for the second, and spent the rest of her life surrounded by an enslaved entourage of descendants and churchmen.

In my great-grandmother's case the church was the one blandly called Christian by its followers and Campbellite by the rival Methodists and Baptists. All three of these sects were in their most exciting period of growth during old Mrs. Oliver's long reign, and their rousing camp meetings of the frontier days had given way to prosperously organized yearly meeting places, often along the ocean or at pleasant lakes.

The Christians went each year to a beach in Pennsylvania, I think. I remember a name which should be clearer to me, something like Elmwood or Elmhurst. It was there that the whole family spent their summers, in a huge wooden house on the shore from which, as far as our apocrypha recount, the grandmother ran the show not only for the stream of second and third generations of Olivers but for the whole church.

She was a small woman, of boundless enthusiasm and fire, who exhausted everybody but herself by assuming that they were one tenth as energetic as she. She was better bred and read than most of the Irish refugees of that period, especially the women, but some of her forthright prescriptions for herself and others belied her gentle upbringing, and she embarrassed plain hell out of her associates, especially the young ones like my mother.

One of her main sources of energy, she was proud to state clearly, was her nightly salt enema.

The word alone was enough to humiliate the genteel

adolescents who must hear it, but her use of them to provide it for her was a social cross almost past bearing, and one which they paid gladly from their stingy allowances to push off on their younger and weaker relatives.

Two children a week were deputized by old Mrs. Oliver to run down to the beach, just before bedtime, and bring back a quart pitcher filled with salt water, which was left at her bedroom door. My mother earned money from her older cousins for several summers, being young and penniless otherwise, to take their turns at this nightly trot, and in turn passed out a few bribes to be able to go when her favorite, Mary the Family Belle, was on duty too.

Together the girls would run down to the silent beach, the nasty pitcher hidden under a cape, and then slip off their shoes and run into the black water. It was wonderful, my mother said, until they must go back to the house with the sea water, making sure that exactly one quart remained in the pitcher when, disdainful and tittering, they put it beside their grandmother's door.

Apparently Mrs. Oliver gave herself an enema each night with it, which she retained until the next morning . . . to absorb strength from the minerals in it, my mother said deprecatingly, and then always added, "She was a terror."

XXIV

A peck of pickled peppers, Peter Piper
picked.

Anonymous

Perhaps the strong old Irishwoman sought thus, and
even found, in this direct yet devious way, the same virtues which people have long believed to exist in all sea
animals, to add to their virility, their mental keenness,
their longevity.

Oysters have been credited with aphrodisiacal qualities since the days of the first kitchen middens, and although common sense makes it clear that their main aid
to amorous activity is that they are easy to digest and re-
freshingly simple, people still swallow them hopefully
in their pursuit of gonadal bliss.

Eels, more obviously phallic, are also on this optimistic list in many lands, whereas flatter fish like soles and
flounders are depended upon more for intellectual than

for sexual encouragement. This dates at least from the Middle Ages, when sea phosphorus was deemed a "brain food" by the alchemists, and even a couple of centuries ago one of the French kings ordered that all of his ministers and diplomats eat copiously of fish, the better to serve his politics.

For some reason shrimps from the ocean as well as crayfish, the little crustaceans which correctly are not from the sea at all but from fresh water, are firmly believed by people of many lands to possess not only the desirable qualities of the eel and oyster, but most of the other benignities attributed to ocean-going fish. Casanova wrote that perhaps he owed most of his romantic successes to the simple supper his mother demanded the night before his birth in Venice, in 1725—a bowl of hot spiced shrimps. Brillat-Savarin might suggest here, as in his famous story of the dish of eel which he wrote exactly a hundred years later, that the spices acted as subtly, even in Casanova's prenatal conditioning, as did the little *scampi*.

At the end of this anecdote, which has been misquoted for more than two hundred years to prove everything from heresy in the priesthood to pornography in the good professor's own mind, the cook who produced the strangely disturbing meal for a meeting of otherwise saintly divines confessed only that her dish contained a crayfish sauce which had been liberally peppered . . . And since crayfish are so universally credited with exciting virtues, it is useless to speculate whether this artist, formerly a cook in a famous Paris brothel, depended upon a secret powder for her sauce, or anything more than the little fish and plenty of cayenne . . . and of course the eel to begin with!

For people who are open in their search for an excitant at table, some such recipe as the following is typical, combining as it does the mysterious truffle, the purportedly potent crayfish, and the symbolism of the eel:

Receipt for la Cuisine d'Amour

Cut a skinned eel into short pieces, lard them generously with fresh truffles, and bake them in a hot oven for ten minutes, each wrapped in buttered paper. Serve on a bed of crayfish tails which have been stewed in dry white wine and well seasoned with cayenne.

According to ancient rumors, crayfish are helpful to us as a restorative from the very excitements they can induce, and they have long been used in soups and tonics for many kinds of surfeit. This seeming contradiction is as unreasonable as Brillat-Savarin's advising the use of quinine as an "anti-fat," in the face of its powers to goad an appetite, or the very ancient use of doves in soups or pies, to incite love in a person and then later to help him recover and gain new strength . . .

Love is not the only wearisome thing that can be helped and then offset by the canny use of crayfish, though; and some three hundred years ago Elizabethans with such seemingly disparate troubles as asthma and "swell'd legs" were drinking morning and night potions, as I have already noted, made of many herbs and juices bound together with "The Tails of 12 live Crawfish with the Shell on them, Bruised in a Marble Mortar. . . ."

Another recipe, this time labeled plainly A Restorative, is recommended by Brillat-Savarin for "people of unstable and vacillating temperament, and for all those, in a word, who grow tired for no apparent reason":

Take a knuckle of veal of not less than two pounds, cut it in quarters lengthwise, flesh and bone, and brown it with four sliced onions and a handful of watercress. When it is almost cooked through, add three bottles of water, and let the whole boil for two hours, taking care to replace whatever evaporates. Add pepper and salt in moderation.

Pound separately three old pigeons and twenty-five very fresh crayfish. Mix well and brown nicely in enough butter to keep from sticking. Add the veal bouillon, cook rapidly for one hour, strain, and drink in the mornings only, two hours before breakfast.

According to the benign old Frenchman, he prepared this broth for two writers, who "used [it] as directed, and have never had reason to regret it. The poet, who before was no more than elegiac, has become romantic. The lady, who had nothing to her credit but one fairly colorless novel filled with catastrophes, has written a second one which is much better, and which ends with a happy marriage. In both cases a marked increase in creative strength. . . ."

Was it the crayfish, those curly-tailed inciters to renascence? Was it perhaps the sharp, crisp freshness of the watercress, which Homeric banqueters wore almost as commonly as parsley in wreaths upon their heads, to keep themselves clear of the fumes and fogs of drinking? Was it the reassurance of following a prescribed rhythm, an orderly pattern with all the magic in it of other more religious rites which have long strengthened men?

A certain gesture at a certain time, the inner warmth of the mild tonic bath, the trustful obedience—healing, it is called!

Conclusion

Men freely believe that which they
desire.

Julius Caesar

And here are two recipes, perhaps to prove this book's
possible excuse.

For a Consumpsion

Take 30 garden snails & 30 Earth worms of middling sise,
bruise ye snails & wash them & ye worms in fair waters, cut
ye worms in peices. Boil these in a quart of Spring water to
a pint. Pour it boiling on 2 ounses of Candied Eringo root
sliced thin. When it is cold strain it thro a fine flannel bag.
Take a quarter of a pint of it warm, with an Equal Quantity
of Cows' milk till well, at twilight.

Truth . . . Faith . . . Miracles!

Come tonight to the Mission of Divine Healing, where the
Deliverance of Man will be announced! There will be the
Laying on of Hands!! Testimonies of Heavenly Cures will be
Made Aloud!!! Come with Faith, and you will find Peace,
Health, and Happiness! Free Admission!!!

The first receipt is from the journal kept by a London apothecary in Shakespeare's time. The second is from a handbill thrust at me once in France by a tall man dressed in rough, thick clothes.

It was night. Down the side street from which he darted now and then with his bunch of flimsy papers I could hear the quavering of a dismal hymn. It sounded strange in the dark, sung perhaps by five or six ancient women, and its Wesleyan measures were doubly foreign in that Catholic town where Campra had been born and where schoolboys whistled phrases from the Jerusalem Psalter as much as they did from the latest rock-and-roll. But the handbill was no stranger to me than the other recipe, for both spoke of incantation, and mystery, and ageless faith: the essentials of healing.